Build Your Dark Web Mastery with Linux

A Complete Guide to Setting Up and Operating an Onion Site

Written by, Lynne Kolestar

Table of Contents

Introduction

The internet is often perceived as a vast and open space where information is readily accessible to anyone. However, this perception only scratches the surface of what truly exists online. Beneath the familiar websites and search engines that most people use daily lies a much larger, more concealed portion of the web. This unseen territory is divided into the surface web, deep web, and dark web—each playing a distinct role in the online ecosystem. To understand the dark web and its significance, it's essential to first understand how these layers of the internet differ.

What is the Dark Web?

The dark web is a part of the internet that is deliberately hidden and can only be accessed through specific software, such as Tor (The Onion Router). The Dark Web is often conflated with illicit activity, but in reality, the dark web encompasses a wide range of content—some of which is perfectly legal and ethical, while other parts facilitate criminal activities. To fully grasp the dark web's role, it's necessary to distinguish it from the surface web and the deep web.

Overview of the surface web, deep web, and dark web

The surface web refers to the publicly accessible portion of the internet that is easily indexed by search engines like Google, Bing, and Yahoo. This includes websites such as news outlets, social media platforms, online stores, and blogs. These sites are part of the visible internet and are subject to the legal regulations of both the country where they are hosted and general internet governance. Despite its prominence, the surface web constitutes only about 4% of the entire internet.

The deep web refers to all parts of the internet that are not indexed by search engines and cannot be accessed through standard web browsers. This includes private databases, academic resources, medical records, subscription services, and company intranets. The deep web is vast and, unlike the dark web, is not intentionally hidden; rather, it contains information that is kept private for security or organizational reasons. Most online users unknowingly interact with the deep web when accessing things like email accounts or online banking.

The dark web is a small portion of the deep web that has been intentionally hidden and is accessible only through special software like Tor, which anonymizes users' identities and locations by routing their connection through multiple encrypted layers. Websites on the dark web use an **".onion"** domain and can host anything from whistleblower forums and political activism sites to black markets for illegal goods. The anonymity offered by the dark web makes it attractive for both those seeking privacy and those engaged in illegal activity, leading to its notorious reputation.

While the surface web is the most familiar and visible, the deep web encompasses the bulk of the internet, and the dark web represents a hidden, anonymized space within that framework. This layered structure of the web creates a complex environment where privacy, secrecy, and criminal activities intersect, giving rise to both legitimate and illicit uses of the dark web. Understanding this distinction is key to navigating and mastering the dark web safely and responsibly.

How onion sites work and why they are significant

Onion sites, also known as Tor hidden services, are websites that can only be accessed via the Tor (The Onion Router) network. Unlike regular websites on the surface web that use standard domain names and IP addresses, onion sites use ".**onion**" addresses and rely on multiple layers of encryption to ensure user anonymity. This makes them an essential part of the dark web, where privacy and anonymity are paramount. The name "**onion**" comes from the layered approach to encryption, which is akin to peeling an onion, with each layer representing a node that obscures the origin and destination of data.

When accessing an onion site, a user's connection is routed through several volunteer-run servers, or nodes, in the Tor network. Each node decrypts only enough information to pass the data to the next node, effectively masking the user's IP address and making it nearly impossible to trace the origin of the request. This multi-layered encryption process ensures that both the user and the website remain anonymous, unlike traditional browsing where IP addresses are easily trackable. The sites themselves are also hosted on the Tor network, which means that their location (the server's IP address) is obscured, preventing tracking or takedown by external entities.

Onion sites are significant for several reasons. First and foremost, they provide a secure platform for users who require anonymity, such as whistleblowers, activists, and journalists working in authoritarian regimes where freedom of speech is restricted. These sites can serve as safe havens for individuals to share information, organize protests, or expose government and corporate wrongdoing without fear of being identified or targeted. The significance of onion sites extends beyond personal privacy to the broader context of civil liberties and the free flow of information.

However, onion sites are also notorious for being used for illegal activities. Dark web marketplaces often use onion sites to sell drugs, weapons, stolen data, and other illicit goods, making law enforcement efforts to combat cybercrime more challenging. The anonymity offered by these sites attracts not only privacy advocates but also criminals who wish to avoid detection. Despite this, onion sites play a dual role in the digital world: they are powerful tools for both protecting human rights and enabling illicit activities. Understanding how onion sites work is crucial for anyone interested in the dark web, whether they are seeking to ensure their own privacy or investigate the darker corners of the internet.

Legal considerations and ethical use of the dark web

The dark web has long been associated with illegal activities such as drug trafficking, arms dealing, and hacking services. However, not everything on the dark web is illegal, and there are legitimate reasons for using it. Understanding the legal considerations surrounding the dark web is crucial for anyone considering its use. While it's not illegal to access the dark web or use the Tor network in most countries, many activities conducted on the dark web may violate local, national, or international laws. Engaging with illegal marketplaces, purchasing contraband, or participating in activities that violate copyright laws or cybersecurity regulations can result in severe legal consequences, including criminal charges.

One of the core legal issues of the dark web is the difficulty of regulating anonymous communication. While the dark web provides users with a high level of anonymity, it also attracts criminal activity, including illegal marketplaces, malware distribution, and illicit networks. Many individuals met on the dark web through social media and other platforms are often involved in criminal activities. Law enforcement agencies such as the FBI, Europol, and others continuously monitor dark web activity, targeting individuals engaged in illegal actions. Users should be aware that, although anonymity is a key feature of the dark web, it is not absolute—authorities have developed sophisticated tools to track illegal activity and unmask users. As a result, individuals participating in illicit activities may face arrest and conviction, as seen with many dark web users involved in illegal transactions or operations. For example, even using the Tor browser without a VPN can be detected, and attempting to engage in illegal activities, such as hiring someone to commit a crime, can lead to serious legal consequences.

Beyond legal concerns, ethical considerations must also be taken into account when navigating the dark web. While it offers a space for anonymity, which can be beneficial for individuals such as whistleblowers, journalists, or people living under oppressive regimes, the dark web is also home to a wide range of harmful and unethical activities. For example, users may come across child exploitation materials, counterfeit goods, or services that are explicitly designed to harm others, like hitman services or illegal hacking tools. Being an ethical user of the dark web requires actively avoiding these darker aspects and using the platform in ways that promote privacy and free expression without contributing to criminal enterprises.

For many, the dark web serves as an essential tool for maintaining privacy and free speech in environments where such freedoms are restricted. It can be used to protect identity, communicate securely, and share sensitive information without fear of censorship or retribution. However, balancing this freedom with ethical responsibility is key. Users must ensure they are not enabling illegal activities and should always use the dark web with a clear understanding of both its positive uses and its potential for harm. By practicing caution, respecting the law, and adhering to ethical principles, users can harness the dark web for good while avoiding its darker, more dangerous elements.

Why Linux for Onion Sites?

Linux is often the preferred operating system for hosting onion sites on the dark web due to its exceptional security, stability, and flexibility. These characteristics make Linux a powerful tool for maintaining anonymity and safeguarding data, which are crucial for dark web operations. The operating system allows users to securely host websites while maintaining privacy and protecting their identity. Its strong architecture limits user permissions, promotes robust security practices, and resists malware and security breaches, which are essential for ensuring confidentiality and data integrity for both site operators and visitors.

In addition to its security features, Linux offers excellent stability and reliability, making it ideal for hosting onion sites that require consistent uptime and performance. Linux-based servers are known for their ability to run for long periods without issues, ensuring that sites remain accessible at all times. The open-source nature of Linux also allows for complete customization, enabling site operators to tailor the system to their specific needs, configure advanced security tools, and install privacy-enhancing software like Tor. This flexibility ensures that users can adapt to the evolving privacy landscape, making Linux a trusted platform for creating and maintaining secure and anonymous online presences on the dark web.

The advantages of using Linux for security, privacy, and control

Linux stands out as one of the most secure operating systems available, and this makes it an ideal choice for individuals and organizations that prioritize privacy and control over their digital environments. The architecture of Linux, combined with its open-source nature and robust security features, offers a high level of protection that is unmatched by many other operating systems. These advantages make Linux the go-to platform for users seeking to safeguard their data, maintain their anonymity, and have full control over their systems and networks.

Enhanced Security Features

One of the most significant advantages of using Linux is its built-in security features. Linux is designed with a security-first mindset, utilizing a strong permission-based system that restricts access to critical parts of the operating system. Unlike other operating systems, Linux operates under the principle of "least privilege," meaning that users and processes are only granted the minimal level of access needed to perform specific tasks. This helps prevent unauthorized access and limits the damage that can be done in the event of a breach.

Additionally, Linux is less prone to common security

vulnerabilities like malware and viruses. Because it is an open-source platform, security flaws are quickly identified and patched by a global community of developers, reducing the window of vulnerability. The collaborative nature of the Linux community ensures that security updates are released promptly and regularly. Compared to other operating systems, this level of proactive security ensures that Linux remains a strong operating system for users who prioritize cybersecurity.

Privacy Protection

For users who value their privacy, Linux offers significant advantages over more mainstream operating systems. Because it is open-source, Linux allows users to scrutinize every line of code, ensuring there are no hidden backdoors or surveillance mechanisms. This transparency is essential for users who want to ensure their personal data remains private and secure. Furthermore, many Linux distributions are designed with privacy in mind, offering tools and configurations that help protect user anonymity while browsing, emailing, and communicating online.

Linux also offers robust support for privacy-enhancing technologies that are available at no cost. For example, users can easily install and configure Tor, a popular tool for browsing the dark web anonymously, or VPNs (Virtual Private Networks) to encrypt internet traffic. Additionally, Linux can be used with tools like cryptsetup for disk encryption, ensuring that sensitive data remains safe even if the device is lost or stolen. These features make Linux an ideal choice for anyone looking to maintain a high level of privacy while using their system.

Complete Control Over the System

Linux is a highly customizable operating system, allowing users to have full control over their environment. Whether you're an experienced system administrator or a casual user, Linux enables you to modify almost every aspect of the system, from user permissions to security settings and even the kernel itself. This level of control is particularly important for individuals who want to ensure their system meets their specific security and privacy needs.

For example, Linux allows users to choose which software is installed and which services are enabled, providing the ability to minimize the attack surface by running only essential services. Furthermore, the flexibility of Linux means users can fine-tune firewall settings, configure encryption protocols, and tailor their operating environment to suit their personal or organizational needs. The ability to directly manage system resources, security protocols, and privacy tools makes Linux an unmatched choice for users who want to be in complete control of their computing experience.

Stability and Minimalist Approach

Linux is also known for its stability and minimalist approach. Many Linux distributions are designed to be lightweight, reducing the likelihood of performance issues that can lead to vulnerabilities or system crashes. This stability is especially important for security-focused environments, where uptime and reliability are essential. By running a streamlined version of Linux with only the necessary services and features, users can significantly reduce the risk of encountering security issues or performance degradation over time.

Linux offers unparalleled advantages when it comes to security, privacy, and control. Its strong security features, open-source nature, and ability to customize every aspect of the system make it the ideal choice for users who want to protect their data, maintain their anonymity, and have full control over their computing environment. Whether you're securing personal information, browsing anonymously, or configuring a secure server, Linux empowers users to safeguard their digital lives with greater confidence and flexibility than any other operating system.

Differences between Linux and other operating systems in dark web hosting

When it comes to dark web hosting, Linux stands out from

other operating systems, particularly in terms of security, customizability, and privacy. Unlike other operating systems like Windows or macOS, Linux is a cost-free and open-source platform, which means its source code is accessible for review and modification. This transparency ensures that there are no hidden backdoors or surveillance mechanisms, which is crucial for users seeking to remain anonymous on the dark web. Additionally, Linux offers more control over system resources and configuration, enabling users to fine-tune their systems to maximize privacy and security. This level of customization is not as easily achievable with other operating systems, which often come with pre-configured settings that limit control and flexibility.

Another key difference is the stability and performance of Linux compared to other operating systems. Linux-based servers are known for their high performance and ability to run for extended periods with minimal maintenance. In contrast, operating systems like Windows may require frequent updates, restarts, and system optimizations, which can lead to vulnerabilities or interruptions in service. Linux also tends to be more lightweight and resource-efficient, making it a preferred choice for hosting onion sites that demand uptime and continuous operation.

Furthermore, Linux's robust security architecture, including its strong permission and access control mechanisms, makes it a safer option for dark web hosting. While Windows and macOS may be susceptible to more frequent attacks due to their larger user bases and broader attack surface, Linux remains less targeted and more resilient against malicious intrusions, making it the optimal choice for users who require high levels of security and reliability on the dark web.

Chapter 1: Understanding the Dark Web and Onion Routing

The History of Tor and Onion Routing

Origins of the Tor network and its purpose

The Tor network originated in the mid-1990s, initially developed by the U.S. Navy for the purpose of enhancing online anonymity and secure communications. The primary goal was to create a tool that would allow government personnel, military officials, and intelligence agencies to communicate covertly over the internet without revealing their location or identity. The project was built on earlier concepts of onion routing, a technique that involves encrypting data multiple times and routing it through a network of relay nodes. Each relay decrypts one layer of encryption, making it difficult for any single node in the chain to trace the origin or destination of the data. This method of anonymization would provide a way for sensitive communications to remain private and secure, even in a globally connected and easily surveilled online environment.

In the early 2000s, the Tor network was made publicly available as open-source software under the development of Roger Dingledine, Nick Mathewson, and Paul Syverson, who continued to build upon the original military framework. The decision to release Tor to the public was driven by the recognition that the need for online privacy and security extended beyond government and military use. Journalists, activists, and ordinary citizens living under oppressive regimes also needed a secure means to communicate without fear of surveillance or censorship. Tor's open-source nature allowed anyone to use, improve, and audit the network, making it a cornerstone of digital privacy. Today, the Tor network continues to serve as a critical tool for maintaining anonymity online, providing access to onion sites and allowing individuals to browse the internet free from censorship and surveillance.

Onion Routing vs. Blockchain: Ensuring Privacy, Anonymity, and Security

Onion routing is a sophisticated privacy-enhancing technique that ensures anonymity by encrypting data multiple times and routing it through a network of distributed nodes, known as relays. The name "onion routing" comes from the process of layering encryption, where each relay in the network decrypts only one layer of encryption—much like peeling away layers of an onion. This layered approach ensures that no single relay in the network knows both the origin and the final destination of the data, offering a high level of protection against surveillance and tracking. As the data moves through the network, each relay can only see the previous and next hop in the chain, making it nearly impossible for an outside observer, including the relays themselves, to trace the data back to its source or destination.

The onion routing process begins when a user sends a request that is encrypted multiple times before being sent through a series of randomly selected relays. Each relay decrypts one layer, uncovering the next hop in the chain, until the final relay decrypts the last layer and forwards the data to its destination. This decentralized routing system ensures that the data remains anonymous, with no single point in the chain possessing full knowledge of the communication path. Even if one relay is compromised or monitored, the encryption and the way the data is routed maintain privacy and security. Onion routing's decentralized nature and layered encryption make it a powerful tool for preserving anonymity on the internet, especially when accessing sensitive services such as onion sites on the dark web.

Though both onion routing and blockchain rely on decentralized networks and cryptographic techniques, they serve fundamentally different purposes and operate in distinct ways. Onion routing is primarily designed for ensuring privacy and anonymity during communication. It secures user data by masking its origin and destination through multiple layers of encryption, which is essential for users seeking to protect their identity while browsing anonymously or accessing hidden services. A prime example of this is the Tor network, which enables secure and anonymous internet access, making it an invaluable tool for users of the dark web.

Blockchain, on the other hand, is a distributed ledger technology designed to **securely record and publicly verify transactions** across a network. Data is grouped into blocks, which are cryptographically linked in a chain, and the entire ledger is visible to all participants in the network. Once a transaction is recorded, it becomes immutable, ensuring transparency and security for digital transactions. The primary goal of blockchain is to enable transparency, decentralization, and immutability of records, particularly in applications like cryptocurrencies. While both blockchain and onion routing utilize cryptography and decentralization, onion routing focuses on **ensuring privacy and anonymity during unverified data transmission**, without requiring public or private verification. In contrast, blockchain is designed to create secure and transparent records of verified transactions.

How the Dark Web Works

Layers of encryption in onion routing

The Dark Web operates as a part of the Deep Web, which is not indexed by traditional search engines and can only be accessed through specialized software like Tor. The key to accessing the Dark Web securely lies in its use of onion routing, a technique that layers encryption to protect the privacy and anonymity of users. Onion routing is named after the way data is encrypted in multiple layers, resembling the layers of an onion. Each layer of encryption is decrypted by a different relay node in the network, ensuring that no single node knows the entire path or the origin and destination of the data. This multi-layer encryption helps ensure that communication over the Dark Web remains private, even from those who might be monitoring the network.

When a user sends data over the Dark Web, it is encrypted multiple times before being transmitted through a series of randomly selected nodes or relays in the Tor network. Each relay decrypts only one layer of encryption, revealing the next hop for the data but not its original source or final destination. This process continues until the data reaches its final destination, at which point the last layer of encryption is removed. By using this method, onion routing ensures that no single relay or node can link the user's identity or their communication with the destination, making it difficult for anyone to trace the source or track the data flow. This layered approach provides a strong degree of anonymity and privacy, which is essential for individuals seeking to maintain their confidentiality while browsing or communicating on the Dark Web.

How data travels through the Tor network

Data travels through the Tor network in a highly secure and anonymous manner, thanks to the process known as onion routing. When a user initiates a request through the Tor network, their data is encrypted multiple times, and each layer of encryption is decrypted by a different relay (node) in the network. This process ensures that no single relay knows both the source and the destination of the data, providing a high level of privacy and anonymity for the user.

Here's how data travels through the Tor network step by step:

Layered Encryption: When a user sends data, it is first encrypted multiple times on their device. Each layer of encryption corresponds to a specific relay in the network. The data is encrypted in such a way that it contains instructions for how it should travel through the network but hides its final destination and origin.

Passing Through Relays: The data is then sent through a series of randomly selected relays, known as nodes. Each relay decrypts one layer of encryption and forwards the data to the next relay, while retaining information only about the previous and next nodes in the path. This is similar to peeling off one layer of the "onion" at each hop, revealing the next destination but hiding the rest of the path.

Final Decryption: Once the data has passed through its last relay, the final layer of encryption is removed, and the data is sent to its destination. At this point, the data is fully decrypted, and the request is processed by the intended server or website.

Anonymity and Security: Throughout this journey, no single relay knows the entire path of the data, ensuring that the origin and destination are obscured. This makes it extremely difficult for anyone monitoring the network to trace the data back to the user or determine the final destination. The use of multiple relays and encryption layers creates a robust system that provides a high degree of anonymity and security, which is why Tor is widely used for secure and anonymous browsing, particularly on the Dark Web.

The Tor network's design — using multiple layers of encryption and routing data through a decentralized network of relays — ensures that the communication remains private and that users can maintain their anonymity while browsing or accessing content on the Dark Web.

Why onion sites are different from standard websites

Onion sites differ significantly from standard websites due to the unique infrastructure that supports them and the specialized network they rely on. The key distinction lies in their use of the Tor network and the **.onion** domain extension, which provides a level of anonymity and security that regular websites, typically hosted on the surface web, do not offer.

The .onion Domain and Tor Network: Unlike regular websites that use traditional domain names ending in .com, .org, or .net, onion sites use the **.onion** extension. This domain is not accessible through standard browsers and can only be accessed via the Tor network, which anonymizes traffic by routing it through multiple relays. This ensures that both the users visiting the site and the site owners can remain anonymous, making it significantly harder to trace either party. In contrast, standard websites are usually hosted on regular servers and are typically identifiable by their IP addresses, making it easier to track users' activities and server locations.

Enhanced Privacy and Anonymity: Onion sites are designed to preserve privacy and anonymity. The Tor network uses a method called onion routing, where data is encrypted in multiple layers and sent through several nodes (relays), each of which can only decrypt one layer, revealing the next node in the path. This process ensures that no single relay knows both the origin and destination of the data, protecting the identities of both the user and the site owner. On the other hand, standard websites usually do not provide this level of protection. Although HTTPS can encrypt the data between a user and a website, it does not hide the user's IP address or protect the server's location, which makes it much easier for third parties to monitor and track activities.

Access Restrictions and Content: Onion sites often host content that is restricted or censored on the surface web. They are frequently used for sensitive or illegal activities, but they also serve legitimate purposes, such as protecting free speech in repressive regimes or offering secure communication channels for activists and journalists. Standard websites, on the other hand, are typically subject to traditional regulations and restrictions based on the country or jurisdiction in which they are hosted. While onion sites are often beyond the reach of standard law enforcement, they can be difficult to monitor, providing a degree of resistance to censorship and surveillance that regular websites cannot offer. Additionally, regular search engines like Google do not index or search for **.onion** sites at all, making them virtually invisible to the general public unless accessed through the Tor network itself.

Decentralized Hosting: Many onion sites are hosted on decentralized or private servers, which further protects their users and operators. Since onion sites do not rely on centralized hosting services that can be traced or shut down by authorities, they offer a higher degree of security for both the site owner and visitors. This decentralization is not common on standard websites, where hosting is usually done through commercial providers that can be subpoenaed or pressured to hand over user data.

Onion sites are fundamentally different from standard websites in their use of the Tor network, the **.onion** domain extension, and their focus on privacy, anonymity, and decentralized hosting. These features make them particularly appealing to those who need a higher level of protection from surveillance or censorship, although they also make onion sites a popular destination for illicit activities. Regular search engines do not index **.onion** sites, further contributing to their hidden and secure nature.

Key Use Cases for Onion Sites

Anonymous communication

One of the primary use cases for onion sites is anonymous communication, which is essential for individuals and organizations seeking to protect their privacy while interacting online. Onion sites, accessed through the Tor network, provide a secure, anonymous channel for communication that is resistant to surveillance and censorship. This is particularly important for people in regions with oppressive regimes, where freedom of speech is limited and individuals may face severe consequences for expressing dissenting opinions. Governments and intelligence agencies, including the CIA, also utilize onion sites to ensure secure and anonymous communication. For example, the CIA operates an onion site for secure whistleblowing, allowing individuals to submit sensitive information anonymously without fear of retaliation.

Whistleblowing and Journalism

Onion sites are widely used by whistleblowers to safely leak sensitive information, especially in cases involving government corruption, corporate misconduct, or human rights violations. Platforms like SecureDrop are designed to facilitate this type of communication. SecureDrop allows journalists to securely receive documents and communicate with anonymous sources without revealing their identities or the identities of those providing the information. The system ensures that both parties remain anonymous, preventing retaliation or persecution. High-profile examples include the use of SecureDrop by media outlets like The Washington Post and The Guardian, which have provided a secure avenue for whistleblowers to share confidential materials.

Activism and Political Dissent

Activists and political dissidents in authoritarian countries rely on onion sites to communicate securely and organize without fear of government surveillance. In countries with strict censorship and surveillance, where citizens' internet activities are heavily monitored, onion sites provide a platform for free expression. Platforms like ProPublica's dark web version of their site offer a way for individuals to access news and communicate freely while bypassing internet censorship. The use of onion sites for communication allows protesters and activists to coordinate efforts, share information, and mobilize without putting themselves at risk of being tracked by oppressive governments.

Privacy-focused Email Services

Another key use case for onion sites is anonymous email services, which enable users to send and receive emails without revealing their identity or location. Services such as ProtonMail (which offers an onion site) allow individuals to create encrypted, anonymous email accounts that are accessible only through the Tor network. These services do not require personal information to sign up, making them a popular choice for individuals who want to avoid surveillance, including journalists, activists, and others operating in sensitive or high-risk environments. By utilizing onion sites for email communication, users can ensure that their messages remain private and cannot be intercepted or traced by adversaries.

Secure Messaging and Forums

Onion sites are also used to host secure messaging platforms and discussion forums, providing users with the ability to communicate freely without revealing their identity. Websites like DuckDuckGo (which offers privacy-oriented search services) and TorChat (an anonymous chat service) leverage the Tor network to provide encrypted, anonymous communication. For example, many activists use encrypted messaging boards and forums hosted on onion sites to discuss sensitive topics like protests, political movements, or human rights efforts. These sites allow individuals to express opinions and share ideas without fear of being monitored, making them critical for fostering free speech in restricted environments.

Mental Health and Support Communities

Onion sites also play an important role in mental health support for individuals who may not feel comfortable seeking help through traditional, identifiable means. Websites that provide counseling or support groups can be hosted anonymously on the Tor network, allowing individuals to discuss personal issues, including mental health struggles, without fear of social stigmatization or exposure. The anonymity of onion sites helps people who might otherwise remain silent about their concerns to find the help they need in a secure environment, without having to reveal personal information.

Online Privacy Services

Finally, onion sites are used to offer services that prioritize online privacy. These services include anonymous web browsing, secure file sharing, and VPN services that shield users from surveillance and tracking. Examples like TorGuard provide encrypted, anonymous VPN services through onion sites, helping users protect their browsing history and online activities from prying eyes.

Onion sites are integral to maintaining privacy and freedom of communication in an increasingly surveilled world. Whether used by journalists to receive leaks, activists to organize under oppressive regimes, or individuals seeking mental health support anonymously, onion sites enable secure, anonymous communication across a range of sensitive contexts. These uses highlight the crucial role that the dark web plays in protecting personal privacy and acilitating free expression, even in the face of censorship and government control.

Whistleblowing and freedom of information

Whistleblowing is a vital mechanism for exposing wrongdoing, corruption, or unethical behavior within organizations, governments, and corporations. In today's increasingly connected and surveilled world, ensuring that whistleblowers can act without fear of retaliation or exposure is crucial. Onion sites, accessed through the Tor network, have become a fundamental tool in this regard, enabling secure and anonymous channels for whistleblowers to safely disclose sensitive information. These platforms play a crucial role in promoting transparency and accountability, often shedding light on issues that might otherwise remain hidden.

The Role of Onion Sites in Whistleblowing

Onion sites provide a unique advantage for whistleblowers: anonymity. By routing communications through multiple layers of encryption, onion sites make it nearly impossible for anyone to trace the origin of the information being shared, protecting the identity of the whistleblower. This makes these sites particularly attractive to individuals who are concerned about the potential consequences of revealing secrets or exposing illegal practices within powerful institutions.

One of the most well-known platforms for facilitating secure whistleblowing is SecureDrop, which is used by several high-profile news organizations to receive anonymous tips. SecureDrop ensures that both the whistleblower and the journalist remain anonymous throughout the process, using end-to-end encryption to safeguard communications. By requiring no personal information and providing a secure, anonymous way to communicate, SecureDrop helps prevent potential retaliation or harm to those sharing confidential information.

High-Profile Examples of Whistleblowing on Onion Sites

Several well-known examples highlight the importance of onion sites in the whistleblowing process, particularly in cases where the stakes are high, and the need for privacy is critical.

Edward Snowden and the NSA Leaks

One of the most famous whistleblowers in recent history is Edward Snowden, the former NSA contractor who leaked classified information revealing widespread government surveillance programs. While Snowden initially contacted journalists through traditional means, he later used SecureDrop to provide additional classified documents.

SecureDrop allowed him to continue his communication with journalists in complete anonymity, reducing the risk of interception or identification.

Chelsea Manning and WikiLeaks

Chelsea Manning, a former U.S. Army intelligence analyst, disclosed a massive amount of classified material to WikiLeaks, including diplomatic cables, battlefield reports, and videos of military operations. While Manning's case is distinct from typical whistleblowing, as she communicated directly with the organization that published the documents, WikiLeaks itself has been a platform heavily used by whistleblowers to share sensitive information. The organization's use of the dark web, including Tor, has helped shield the identities of numerous whistleblowers over the years.

ProPublica's Dark Web Site

ProPublica, a nonprofit investigative news organization, operates an onion site to allow anonymous sources to share sensitive information securely. The platform was launched in 2017 and is specifically designed for whistleblowers who want to expose corruption, misconduct, or abuse within government, corporations, or other organizations. By offering an anonymous way to submit documents, ProPublica has helped ensure that important stories reach the public while protecting the safety and privacy of whistleblowers.

Freedom of Information and the Impact of Whistleblowing

Whistleblowing plays a significant role in upholding the principles of freedom of information and transparency. Without access to key information, the public cannot hold governments and organizations accountable for their actions. Onion sites enable the flow of such critical information in an anonymous and secure manner, ensuring that those with access to sensitive data can share it without fear of reprisal.

In some cases, the information revealed by whistleblowers can lead to major changes in policies or laws.

For example:

The Dark Web as a Tool for Journalists and Whistleblowers:

As of 2023, several major publications, including *The New York Times*, maintain dark web portals to allow secure submissions of whistleblower information. These sites enable sources to share confidential data without fear of government surveillance or retaliation. For example, during the Russian invasion of Ukraine, Ukrainian citizens used dark web versions of social media to bypass government censorship, providing crucial real-time updates on the conflict.

Exposing Corruption and Misconduct:

Whistleblowers have used the dark web to expose corporate misconduct, governmental corruption, and human rights violations. These leaks can lead to significant political or social changes. However, the dark web also serves as a double-edged sword, as it facilitates not only critical transparency but also illegal activities, like cybercrime and black-market transactions.

Legal and Ethical Considerations

While onion sites and the Tor network provide critical tools for safeguarding the identity of whistleblowers, the use of these technologies for whistleblowing can raise legal and ethical concerns. Some organizations and governments view whistleblowers as threats to national security or corporate interests, and in some cases, individuals who reveal sensitive information may face legal action or prosecution. The Espionage Act in the U.S., for example, has been used to charge individuals like Snowden and Manning for leaking classified materials.

However, the role of whistleblowers in ensuring accountability and transparency often outweighs these concerns. Many argue that exposing corruption, human rights abuses, or illegal activities is essential for a functioning democracy and that protecting whistleblowers is a fundamental right. To support this, numerous international organizations, including the United Nations and Amnesty

International, advocate for stronger protections for whistleblowers.

The Future of Whistleblowing

As technology continues to evolve, the tools available to whistleblowers will become more sophisticated. Onion sites and the Tor network are likely to remain central to the fight for transparency and accountability. By providing a secure, anonymous means of communication, these platforms help ensure that individuals who are aware of misconduct or corruption can expose it without risking their safety or freedom.

As surveillance technologies become more advanced, it will be increasingly important to have robust systems that protect the privacy and security of whistleblowers. Onion sites are a key component of this, empowering individuals to bring important issues to light and play a vital role in the fight for freedom of information. Whether it's exposing government overreach, corporate corruption, or human rights abuses, the ability to communicate securely and

anonymously is crucial for whistleblowers around the world.

Secure marketplaces

Secure marketplaces on the dark web, often referred to as "darknet markets," are online platforms that provide a space for individuals to buy and sell goods and services anonymously across the world. These marketplaces operate in the Tor network, utilizing the encryption and anonymity features of onion routing to protect the identities of both buyers and sellers. While some darknet marketplaces have gained notoriety for illegal activities, they also play a role in promoting privacy and secure transactions for individuals or businesses who value or require anonymity or are operating in regions with restricted access to goods and services.

How Secure Marketplaces Work

The primary feature of secure marketplaces on the dark web is the level of privacy they provide. Accessing these marketplaces requires the use of the Tor browser, which ensures that both buyers and sellers can remain anonymous by hiding their IP addresses and encrypting their internet traffic through multiple layers of nodes.

Accessing the Marketplace

A user must first connect to the Tor network using the Tor browser, which provides a gateway to onion sites. Darknet marketplaces typically have a **.onion** domain, and these domains are not indexed by traditional search engines, meaning that users must know the specific address to access the site. The marketplaces often appear similar to e-commerce websites, with categories for products, reviews, and user ratings.

Anonymity and Payment

One of the key reasons people turn to darknet marketplaces is the ability to maintain anonymity. In many cases, transactions on these marketplaces are made using cryptocurrencies like Bitcoin, Monero, or Ethereum, which offer additional layers of privacy and security compared to traditional payment methods. By using cryptocurrency, buyers and sellers avoid exposing personal financial details, such as credit card numbers or bank accounts, that could link them to their transactions.

Escrow Services

To add a layer of trust and security, most darknet marketplaces use an escrow system. When a buyer purchases a product, the funds are held in escrow by the marketplace until the buyer confirms that the product has been received. If there is a dispute between the buyer and the seller (for example, the product is not delivered or is not as described), the marketplace can mediate the dispute and refund the buyer's money. This adds an element of consumer protection that is often lacking in the unregulated market.

Product Listings and Reviews

Darknet marketplaces are often organized into categories such as electronics, drugs, services, and digital products. Each listing includes a description of the product, its price (usually in cryptocurrency), and a rating system based on reviews from previous buyers. Reputation plays a crucial role in these markets, as buyers are more likely to purchase from sellers who have positive feedback and a history of successful transactions. This system helps mitigate the risk of fraud or scams, though it is not foolproof.

Security and Encryption

To protect users' data, communication between buyers, sellers, and marketplace administrators is encrypted, preventing third parties from intercepting or reading the messages. In addition, the marketplaces themselves often employ additional security measures, such as two-factor authentication (2FA) or the use of VPNs, to ensure that users' personal information is safeguarded.

Popular Examples of Secure Marketplaces

Some of the most well-known and widely used darknet marketplaces have operated for years, though many have been shut down by law enforcement agencies over time. Despite their frequent takedowns, new marketplaces continue to emerge.

Here are a few examples:

Kraken Market: Following the shutdown of the massive Hydra market, several former Hydra vendors migrated to Kraken, making it one of the significant players in the darknet market space. Kraken has reportedly maintained a high level of security and a large user base, making it a notable market in 2024.

OMG!: This market emerged in 2021 and has grown to be quite popular, largely due to its secure environment and offerings that cater to the same types of illicit goods once provided by Hydra. It's a trusted platform for both vendors and users who seek a secure and efficient transaction environment.

White House Market: Known for its emphasis on security and user anonymity, White House Market was still operational at the end of 2023 and remains one of the more stable platforms for users. It offers a variety of illicit goods, including drugs, stolen data, and fake documents.

Silk Road: Launched in 2011, Silk Road was the first major darknet marketplace that gained international attention. Known primarily for its role in facilitating the sale of illicit goods, especially illegal drugs, Silk Road became infamous as a place where users could buy and sell anonymously. The platform was seized and shut down by the FBI in 2013, and its founder, Ross Ulbricht, was arrested and later sentenced to life in prison. Silk Road's shutdown was a significant moment in the history of dark web marketplaces, but its legacy lives on as a reference point for many of the darknet markets that followed.

AlphaBay: AlphaBay was one of the largest and most successful darknet marketplaces, operating between 2014 and 2017. It offered a wide range of products, from drugs and counterfeit currencies to hacking tools and stolen data. AlphaBay was known for its robust security features and large user base. However, it was taken down by law enforcement in 2017 in a coordinated global operation. Before its takedown, AlphaBay had become a go-to marketplace for those seeking illicit goods on the dark web.

Dream Market: Dream Market was another large and popular marketplace that survived longer than many others, operating from 2013 until 2019. It offered a variety of illegal products, including drugs, fake IDs, and malware. Dream Market was known for being more stable and reliable than some of its competitors, and it had a loyal user base.

However, in 2019, it abruptly shut down, with rumors suggesting that the administrators decided to close the site to avoid a law enforcement crackdown.

Dark Web Marketplaces Today: After the takedowns of major marketplaces like Silk Road and AlphaBay, newer platforms such as White House Market and Versus Market have filled the gap. These marketplaces continue to provide secure, anonymous spaces for individuals to engage in commerce on the dark web, with a variety of products ranging from personal services to illegal goods. The rise of decentralized markets (using blockchain technology) has also been a development in the dark web space, allowing for greater resistance to takedowns.

Legitimate Uses of Secure Marketplaces: While many secure marketplaces on the dark web are associated with illegal activity, there are also legitimate uses for these platforms. The anonymity they provide can be a vital tool for individuals in oppressive regions where freedom of speech, access to information, and the right to privacy are restricted.

Some of the more responsible marketplaces focus on facilitating the exchange of legal goods and services, including:

Privacy-Enhancing Tools: Many dark web marketplaces sell privacy tools such as encrypted messaging services, secure email providers, and VPNs. These services allow individuals to protect their digital communications from surveillance by governments, corporations, and hackers.

Whistleblowing and Journalism: Secure marketplaces can also be used by whistleblowers, journalists, and activists to exchange information, reports, or other materials securely. The anonymity provided by Tor and the marketplace's escrow system ensures that these transactions are protected, reducing the risks associated with exposing corruption or misconduct.

Access to Information and Services in Censored Regions In countries with strict censorship laws, individuals may use darknet marketplaces to access blocked services such as uncensored news, educational resources, or political advocacy groups. The ability to freely access these services without surveillance is a critical function for those living under authoritarian regimes.

Risks and Challenges - Despite the security measures in place, dark web marketplaces are not without risks:

Illegal Activities: The majority of transactions on these marketplaces involve illegal goods, including narcotics, counterfeit products, and stolen data. This raises concerns for law enforcement agencies and governments, leading to frequent crackdowns on these platforms.

Fraud and Scams: While reviews and ratings help mitigate risks, dark web marketplaces are still susceptible to fraud. Unscrupulous sellers may take advantage of the anonymous nature of the platform to scam buyers.

Law Enforcement: Law enforcement agencies worldwide are increasingly focusing on dismantling darknet marketplaces. The use of undercover operations and monitoring of cryptocurrency transactions has led to multiple successful takedowns of large-scale marketplaces.

Secure marketplaces on the dark web provide a space for individuals to trade goods and services anonymously, protected by encryption and the Tor network. While many of these markets facilitate illegal activity, they also serve as a vital tool for privacy-conscious individuals, journalists, activists, and whistleblowers. The continued existence of such marketplaces underscores the ongoing need for secure, anonymous communication channels in a world where digital privacy is constantly under threat. However, their role in promoting illegal activity also poses challenges for governments and law enforcement agencies working to combat cybercrime. The future of dark web marketplaces will depend on the ongoing balance between privacy, security, and the need for regulation.

Chapter 2: Preparing Your Environment

Choosing the Right Linux Distribution

Recommended Linux distros for privacy and security (e.g., Debian, Ubuntu, Tails)

When it comes to selecting the right Linux distribution (distro) for privacy and security, the decision largely depends on the user's specific needs and technical skills. Linux is renowned for its robustness, customization options, and privacy-focused features, making it a popular choice for those who prioritize security. However, not all distributions are created equal when it comes to protecting privacy and ensuring system integrity. Below are some of the most recommended Linux distros for privacy and security, each with its unique strengths.

Tails

Best for: Maximum anonymity and privacy.

Tails (The Amnesic Incognito Live System) is a privacy-focused live Linux distribution designed specifically for anonymity. It routes all internet traffic through the Tor network, ensuring that users' online activities are anonymized. Tails is a live distribution, meaning it runs entirely from a USB stick or DVD, leaving no trace on the system once it is powered off. This makes it an excellent choice for users who need to maintain absolute privacy while working in sensitive or high-risk environments.

Tor Integration: All traffic is automatically routed through Tor, ensuring that users' IP addresses and browsing activities remain anonymous.

Amnesia: Tails does not store data on the machine, and once the system is turned off, all traces are erased, ensuring no remnants are left behind.

Encryption Tools: Tails comes with built-in tools like VeraCrypt and LUKS to securely encrypt data, as well as secure messaging apps like Pidgin and OTR.

USB Persistence: Tails allows users to store encrypted data on the USB drive with persistence, ensuring that essential files and configurations can be saved across reboots.

Tails is ideal for users who need a disposable, secure, and anonymous operating environment. It is widely used by journalists, whistleblowers, and activists in regions with oppressive surveillance.

Debian

Best for: Stable and secure system for everyday use.

Debian is a widely respected Linux distribution known for its stability, security, and commitment to open-source principles. It's the foundation for many other popular distributions, including Ubuntu. Debian's commitment to free software and its rigorous security policies make it a strong choice for those who want a secure Linux system for everyday use while maintaining a high level of control over their privacy.

Security Patches: Debian's security team provides timely security patches for software vulnerabilities, making it a reliable choice for those looking for a system that prioritizes security.

Stable Release: The stable release of Debian is well-tested, ensuring that security updates are applied regularly and the system remains stable and secure.

Minimal Installation: Debian allows for minimal installations, enabling users to avoid unnecessary software and reduce the attack surface of their system.

Trusted Repositories: Debian uses official, well-vetted repositories, reducing the risk of introducing malicious or poorly-maintained software.

Debian is an excellent choice for users who want a solid, reliable, and secure operating system that can be customized to their specific privacy and security needs. It is well-suited for both desktop users and servers.

Ubuntu (with Privacy Adjustments)

Best for: Users who want a user-friendly, secure desktop experience.

Ubuntu is one of the most popular Linux distributions and is known for its ease of use and large user community. While Ubuntu does not come pre-configured for privacy and security by default, it can be easily modified to improve privacy by installing privacy-oriented tools and adjusting system settings. For new Linux users who are looking for a user-friendly environment but still want a secure system, Ubuntu is a good choice.

AppArmor Security Framework: Ubuntu includes AppArmor, a mandatory access control (MAC) system that enforces security policies and prevents applications from performing malicious activities.

Canonical's Commitment to Security: Ubuntu receives regular security updates from Canonical, ensuring that vulnerabilities are patched quickly.

Pre-installed Tools: Ubuntu comes with several essential privacy tools like Gufw (firewall), and users can easily install tools like Tor, VPNs, and encryption software.

Ubuntu Privacy & Security Settings: With some adjustments, such as disabling certain telemetry features and using strong encryption, Ubuntu can be made to offer a solid level of security and privacy.

Ubuntu is ideal for users who are new to Linux and need a system that is secure and easy to maintain, while also having the flexibility to install privacy tools. By making simple adjustments, Ubuntu can be turned into a privacy-conscious operating system.

Whonix

Best for: Users requiring maximum anonymity for internet activities.

Whonix is a privacy-focused Linux distribution designed for users who require an extra layer of anonymity, particularly when using the internet. Whonix works by routing all internet traffic through the Tor network, but it takes this a step further by separating the "workstation" (the part of the system used for browsing and communication) from the "gateway" (the Tor network itself). This unique approach reduces the risk of leaks and ensures that all data is securely anonymized.

Two-VM System: Whonix uses a two-virtual machine (VM) approach. The Whonix Gateway handles all network traffic through Tor, while the Whonix Workstation is where the user interacts with the internet, ensuring that the workstation's IP address is never exposed.

Built-in Anonymity: Since all internet activity is routed through Tor and separated into two distinct VMs, the risk of exposing the user's real IP address is minimized.

Security Focused Software: Whonix comes with privacy and security tools such as the Tor browser, PGP encryption, and secure messaging apps pre-installed.

Isolation: Even if a user were to inadvertently download a malicious file, the isolated VM system ensures that the damage is limited and cannot reach the internet or personal data.

Whonix is ideal for individuals who require high levels of anonymity and need to ensure that their online activities cannot be traced. This makes it a popular choice among journalists, activists, and others operating in high-risk environments.

Qubes OS

Best for: Advanced users needing isolation and compartmentalization

Qubes OS is an advanced security-focused Linux distribution that uses virtualization to isolate different tasks and applications. Each task, from web browsing to email, is run in its own virtual machine (VM), creating a highly secure environment. This approach makes it one of the most secure Linux distributions available, as any vulnerabilities or exploits in one virtual machine do not affect the others.

Isolation of Tasks: Qubes OS isolates each application and service in its own virtual machine (VM), so if one VM is compromised, the others remain secure.

Security-First Design: The OS is designed with security in mind, utilizing Xen-based virtualization and the principle of least privilege.

Integrated Privacy Tools: Qubes OS integrates various privacy tools, including Tor and Whonix, into separate virtual machines, making it ideal for users who need to securely browse the web, communicate, and handle sensitive information.

Granular Control: Users have granular control over which virtual machine can access specific hardware, networks, or other services, providing a high degree of customization for privacy and security.

Qubes OS is ideal for users who have advanced knowledge of Linux and security. It's particularly suited for individuals handling sensitive data or working in high-risk environments, as it offers the highest level of isolation and protection against potential threats.

When choosing a Linux distribution for privacy and security, the decision depends on your needs, technical expertise, and the level of privacy required. Tails and Whonix provide the most robust options for anonymity, making them perfect for journalists, whistleblowers, and activists. For general-purpose use with a strong focus on privacy and security,

Debian and Ubuntu (with privacy tweaks) are excellent options. Advanced users seeking maximum security and isolation can opt for Qubes OS. Regardless of the choice, Linux distributions provide a flexible and powerful platform to safeguard privacy and ensure security in today's increasingly surveilled digital world.

Installing Linux on a dedicated machine or virtual machine

Tails (Live USB) Installation – Dedicated Machine (Live USB):

Download the Tails ISO: Go to Tails website https://tails.boum.org and download the latest stable ISO file.

Create a Bootable USB:

On Windows, use Rufus: Select the Tails ISO and your USB drive, set Partition Scheme to GPT, and File System to FAT32.

On Linux or macOS, use dd:

```
sudo dd if=/path/to/tails.iso of=/dev/sdX bs=4M
status=progress && sync
```

Boot from USB: Insert the USB stick into the machine, restart, and enter the BIOS to select the USB as the primary boot device.

Live Session: Boot into Tails. If needed, enable persistence by creating an encrypted volume on the USB for storing files across sessions.

Tails (Live USB) Installation – Virtual Machine (VM):

Download Tails ISO from the Tails website https://tails.boum.org.

Create a New VM: In VirtualBox or VMware, create a new virtual machine and select the downloaded Tails ISO.

Boot and Run: Start the VM and select the Tails ISO as the boot device. Tails will run as a live OS from the virtual machine.

Debian Installation - Dedicated Machine:

Download the Debian ISO: Go to Debian website https://www.debian.org/ and download the appropriate version (usually "Stable").

Create a Bootable USB: On Windows, use Rufus to create a bootable USB with the Debian ISO.

On Linux/macOS, use dd:

sudo dd if=/path/to/debian.iso of=/dev/sdX bs=4M status=progress && sync

Boot from USB: Insert the USB stick, restart the machine, and boot from USB in BIOS.

Install Debian: Follow the on-screen installation process. Choose your language, region, and set up partitions.

When asked about disk encryption, choose LUKS (Full Disk Encryption) for security.

Install GRUB bootloader when prompted.

Post-installation: After installation, update the system:

```
sudo apt update && sudo apt upgrade
```

Set up firewall, install Tor or VPN tools, and secure your system.

Debian Installation - Virtual Machine (VM): Download

Debian ISO and create a new VM in VirtualBox or VMware.

Create the VM: Choose the downloaded Debian ISO as the boot device.

Install Debian: Follow the installation prompts. Use disk encryption and set up partitions during installation.

Post-installation: After installation, update and install privacy/security tools (e.g., Tor, VPN, firewall).

Ubuntu Installation - Dedicated Machine:

Download the Ubuntu ISO: Go to Ubuntu website https://ubuntu.com/download and download the latest stable version.

Create a Bootable USB: On Windows, use Startup Disk Creator or Rufus to create a bootable USB.

On Linux/macOS, use dd:

```
sudo dd if=/path/to/ubuntu.iso of=/dev/sdX bs=4M status=progress && sync
```

Boot from USB: Insert the USB stick into the machine, reboot, and select the USB as the primary boot device.

Install Ubuntu: Follow the installation prompts. Choose your language, set up partitions, and select full disk encryption when prompted.

Install updates and necessary software after installation.

Post-installation: Install privacy tools like Tor, configure firewall, disable unwanted services, and adjust telemetry settings for privacy.

Ubuntu Installation - Virtual Machine (VM): Download Ubuntu ISO and create a new VM in VirtualBox or VMware.

Create the VM: Choose the Ubuntu ISO as the boot device.

Install Ubuntu: Follow the same installation steps as on a dedicated machine, using encryption where possible.

Post-installation: Install updates and security/privacy tools as needed.

Whonix Installation (VM) - Dedicated Machine (Advanced Setup)

Whonix is primarily designed for virtualization. A dedicated machine setup requires two VMs (Whonix Gateway and Workstation). We recommend running it in VirtualBox or KVM.

Virtual Machine (VM) - Download Whonix ISO files

Go to Whonix website https://www.whonix.org/ and download both the Whonix Gateway and Workstation images.

Create the VMs

In VirtualBox or KVM, create two VMs. One for the Whonix Gateway (which routes all traffic through Tor) and one for the Workstation.

Set the Gateway VM's network adapter to "NAT" and the Workstation VM's network adapter to "Internal Network".

Install Whonix: Import the downloaded ISO files for both Gateway and Workstation into VirtualBox or KVM.

Start both VMs and follow the installation process.

Network Setup: Ensure the Workstation VM is connected to the Gateway VM for all internet traffic.

Qubes OS Installation - Dedicated Machine:

Download Qubes OS ISO: Go to the Qubes OS website https://www.qubes-os.org/ and download the latest ISO version.

Create a Bootable USB: Use Rufus on Windows or dd on Linux/macOS to create a bootable USB with the Qubes ISO.

Boot from USB: Insert the USB stick, reboot the machine, and select USB as the primary boot device in BIOS.

Install Qubes OS: Follow the on-screen installation process.

Choose to partition your disk and enable full disk encryption during setup.

Post-installation: After installation, configure the security settings, create and manage virtual machines (qubes), and set up Qubes-specific tools.

Qubes OS Installation - Virtual Machine (VM): Download Qubes OS ISO and create a new VM in VirtualBox or VMware (Qubes is designed for physical installation but can be tested in a VM with limited functionality).

Create the VM: Allocate sufficient resources and use the downloaded ISO for installation.

Install Qubes OS: Follow the installation prompts. Set up disk encryption and the virtualization configuration.

Post-installation: After installation, manage qubes and configure network settings for isolation.

Setting Up a Secure Environment

Basic Linux command-line skills

Here are some basic Linux commands that you can use across the different Linux distributions for dark web-related activities (using distros like Debian, Ubuntu, Tails, etc.). These commands are generally applicable for privacy, security, and maintaining anonymity when working with Linux in the context of dark web usage.

System Information

uname -a: Displays detailed information about the system's kernel and architecture.
uname -a

df -h: Shows disk space usage, helpful for monitoring storage use.
df -h

free -h: Displays memory usage, great for keeping track of system resources.
free -h

uptime: Shows how long the system has been running since

the last boot.
uptime

top: Displays the currently running processes and their resource usage in real-time.
top

Package Management

sudo apt update: Updates the list of available packages (for Debian-based systems like Ubuntu and Tails).
sudo apt update

sudo apt upgrade: Upgrades all installed packages to the latest version.
sudo apt upgrade

sudo apt install <package>: Installs a specific package, e.g., tor for Tor installation.
sudo apt install tor

sudo apt remove <package>: Removes a specific package.
sudo apt remove tor

Network Commands

ping <domain or IP>: Tests network connectivity. Useful to check whether Tor or dark web services are accessible.

ping example.com

ifconfig: Displays network interface configuration, helpful to check the IP addresses.
ifconfig

netstat -tuln: Displays active network connections and listening ports. Can be useful to monitor traffic.
netstat -tuln

tor: Starts the Tor process (if installed). Important for accessing the Tor network.
tor

File Management

ls: Lists files and directories in the current directory.
ls

cd <directory>: Changes the current directory.
cd /path/to/directory

mkdir <directory_name>: Creates a new directory.
mkdir darkweb_sites

rm <file>: Deletes a file.
rm sensitive_data.txt

cp <source> <destination>: Copies files or directories.

```
cp file1.txt /home/user/backup/
```

Security and Permissions

chmod: Changes file permissions. Use it to secure files with sensitive data.
```
chmod 600 private_key.pem  # Restricts read/write to only the file owner
```

chown: Changes the owner of a file or directory.
```
sudo chown user:user sensitive_data.txt
```

sudo: Executes a command with superuser privileges.
```
sudo apt install tor
```

firejail: A tool to restrict programs to a specific environment, improving privacy by sandboxing applications. (Useful in Tails and other privacy-focused distros.)
```
firejail --private=~/sandbox/ tor
```

Data Encryption and Privacy Tools

gpg --gen-key: Generates a new GPG encryption key. Useful for securely encrypting sensitive communications.
```
gpg --gen-key
```

gpg --encrypt --recipient <email> file.txt: Encrypts a file for a specific recipient using their public GPG key.

gpg --encrypt --recipient user@example.com file.txt

gpg --decrypt file.txt.gpg: Decrypts a file encrypted with GPG.
gpg --decrypt file.txt.gpg

Anonymity and Encryption

tor: Runs the Tor process (if installed), crucial for using the Tor network and accessing **.onion** sites.
tor

torsocks: Wraps an application with Tor to ensure it uses the Tor network.
torsocks curl example.onion

onioncat: A tool that lets you use **.onion** services as if they were local addresses (via a virtual private network).
onioncat -v

Searching the Dark Web

curl: A command-line tool for transferring data with URLs. Can be used to access **.onion** sites.

curl --socks5 127.0.0.1:9050 http://example.onion

lynx: A text-based web browser. Can be used to browse **.onion** websites in a terminal.
lynx http://example.onion

wget: Downloads content from the web. Useful for downloading files from **.onion** sites.
wget --no-check-certificate --quiet http://example.onion/file.txt

System Maintenance and Updates

sudo apt autoremove: Removes unnecessary packages and dependencies.
sudo apt autoremove

sudo apt clean: Cleans up downloaded package files that are no longer needed.
sudo apt clean

sudo reboot: Reboots the system.
sudo reboot

Privacy-Focused Browsing

torbrowser-launcher: If using a Tor browser on Debian/Ubuntu, this command launches the Tor browser safely.
torbrowser-launcher

System Logs

journalctl: Displays logs from the systemd journal, which includes logs for Tor, firewall, and other services.
journalctl -u tor

Securing your system: firewall, updates, and encryption

Securing your Linux system is crucial, especially when using it for privacy-focused activities, including accessing the dark web. Below are steps on how to secure your system using Debian, Ubuntu, and Tails. We'll cover firewall configuration, keeping the system up to date, and implementing encryption.

Firewall Setup - A firewall helps protect your system by filtering incoming and outgoing traffic, blocking potential attackers.

Debian / Ubuntu: Both Debian and Ubuntu typically use UFW (Uncomplicated Firewall) to manage firewall rules.

Install and Enable UFW - Install UFW (if not already installed):

```
sudo apt update
```

```
sudo apt install ufw
```

Enable UFW to block all incoming traffic and allow outgoing traffic (default policy):

```
sudo ufw default deny incoming
```

```
sudo ufw default allow outgoing
```

```
sudo ufw enable
```

Allow specific services, for example, SSH (if you need remote access):

```
sudo ufw allow ssh
```

Check the status of UFW:

```
sudo ufw status
```

Disable UFW (if needed):

```
sudo ufw disable
```

Tails: Tails automatically configures a firewall that blocks all incoming connections by default, only allowing outbound traffic via Tor.

Check firewall status: Tails uses iptables by default, and the firewall is automatically enabled in live mode.

You can check the firewall status with:

sudo iptables -L

Changing firewall settings: You can modify firewall rules in Tails using iptables commands, but the system is designed to be as secure as possible with default settings, so manual changes are generally unnecessary unless specific adjustments are required.

Updating Your System

Regular updates are essential to keep your system secure by patching known vulnerabilities and bugs.

Debian / Ubuntu - Update Package Index:

sudo apt update

Upgrade Installed Packages:

sudo apt upgrade

Perform Full System Upgrade (including distribution upgrades):

sudo apt dist-upgrade

Remove Unnecessary Packages: After upgrades, remove old, unnecessary packages:

sudo apt autoremove

Enable Unattended Upgrades (optional for automatic security updates):

sudo apt install unattended-upgrades

sudo dpkg-reconfigure --priority=low unattended-upgrades

Tails - Update Tails:

Tails provides a built-in tool to update the system, which includes security updates for the live environment.

When you boot Tails, it will prompt you to install updates if available. You can install them directly from the "Applications" menu.

Manual Updates - If needed, you can update specific packages via the terminal:

sudo apt update

```
sudo apt upgrade
```

However, because Tails is designed as a live system, updates are typically only applied when booting from the persistent storage or during a fresh Tails release update.

Encryption

Encryption helps protect the confidentiality of your data by making it unreadable to unauthorized users. This is especially critical when dealing with sensitive information on the dark web.

Debian / Ubuntu - Encrypting a File or Directory:

GPG (GNU Privacy Guard) is commonly used to encrypt files in Linux. You can encrypt files with a recipient's public key, ensuring that only the recipient can decrypt them.

Generate a GPG key pair:

```
gpg --gen-key
```

Encrypt a file:

```
gpg --encrypt --recipient recipient@example.com
sensitive_file.txt
```

Decrypt a file:

```
gpg --decrypt sensitive_file.txt.gpg
```

Full Disk Encryption (FDE) during Installation: Both Debian and Ubuntu allow you to set up full disk encryption during installation, which ensures that your entire system is encrypted and protected by a passphrase.

Steps for Full Disk Encryption (on installation):

Select Encrypt the new installation for security during the installation process.

You will be prompted to choose a passphrase that will be required to access your system each time it boots.

Tails:

Tails provides built-in disk encryption features as part of its default setup for preserving privacy and security.

Persistent Storage Encryption (Only available in Tails when you use persistent storage to save data across sessions):

During boot, you can choose to create encrypted persistent storage.

This allows you to save your data securely across sessions, and it is encrypted by default using LUKS (Linux Unified Key Setup).

Encrypting Files in Tails:

GPG Encryption works in Tails the same way as in other Linux distributions:

gpg --encrypt --recipient recipient@example.com sensitive_file.txt

gpg --decrypt sensitive_file.txt.gpg

Tails also integrates VeraCrypt for volume encryption, which is useful for creating and mounting encrypted containers for sensitive files.

Ensuring Secure Boot and System Integrity

Debian / Ubuntu - Secure Boot: If your machine supports Secure Boot (which protects against rootkits and unauthorized operating system loaders), ensure it's enabled in the BIOS/UEFI settings. Ubuntu supports Secure Boot natively.

To check if Secure Boot is enabled:

mokutil --sb-state

AppArmor: Ubuntu uses AppArmor for application-level security. Ensure it is enabled:

sudo systemctl enable apparmor

sudo systemctl start apparmor

Tails:

Tails automatically disables Secure Boot since it's a live distribution designed to run on various machines, and it might not be compatible with Secure Boot. However, for extra security, always ensure you are using the official Tails ISO file obtained from their official website.

Using Privacy-Focused Tools

Tor: For anonymity, Tor is vital. Make sure that Tor is always running when accessing the dark web.

Start Tor:

sudo service tor start

Verify Tor is Running:

sudo service tor status

Installing and using a VPN with Tor for added protection

Using a VPN in combination with Tor adds an additional layer of protection by hiding your IP address before your traffic enters the Tor network. This can further help anonymize your online activities, especially when accessing sensitive information through the dark web. Below are instructions on how to install and use a VPN with Debian, Ubuntu, and Tails for added protection.

Installing and Using a VPN with Tor on Debian / Ubuntu

Step 1: Install a VPN (OpenVPN)

First, you need to install a VPN client on your Debian or Ubuntu system. One of the most common and widely supported VPN clients is OpenVPN.

Install OpenVPN: Open a terminal and install OpenVPN with the following command:

```
sudo apt update

sudo apt install openvpn
```

Get Your VPN Configuration File: To connect to a VPN, you will need a configuration file (usually .ovpn format) provided by your VPN service provider. Download this file from the VPN provider's website or portal.

Start the VPN Connection - Once the configuration file is ready, use the following command to start the VPN:

```
sudo openvpn --config /path/to/your-vpn-config-file.ovpn
```

Replace /path/to/your-vpn-config-file.ovpn with the actual path to the configuration file you downloaded.

Enter your VPN login credentials if prompted.

Verify the VPN Connection - To check if your VPN is working, you can use the following command to see your current IP address:

```
curl ifconfig.me
```

This should return the IP address provided by your VPN, not your original IP.

Step 2: Install Tor

Next, install Tor to ensure your internet traffic is routed through the Tor network after passing through the VPN.

Install Tor:

sudo apt install tor

Start the Tor Service - Start the Tor service with the following command:

sudo systemctl start tor

Verify the Tor Service - To ensure that Tor is running properly, check its status:

sudo systemctl status tor

Access the Tor Network - Once Tor is running, you can use Tor Browser or route your web traffic through Tor using tools like curl.

To route traffic through Tor, use:

torsocks curl https://check.torproject.org

This command checks if your connection is using Tor.

Step 3: Routing Your Traffic Through VPN and Tor (Double VPN)

By default, traffic is routed from your computer to the VPN first, then to Tor. To ensure the VPN is being used with Tor, simply connect to the VPN first, and then use Tor.

Your data will go through the following process:

VPN -> Tor -> Internet

This ensures that your VPN hides your real IP address, and then Tor encrypts and anonymizes your traffic further.

Using a VPN with Tor on Tails

Tails is designed to prioritize privacy and security, so it routes all traffic through Tor by default. However, you can still use a VPN with Tor in Tails to add an additional layer of security.

Step 1: Start Tails and Connect to the VPN

Boot into Tails: Boot your computer with a Tails USB stick.

Open the VPN Configuration Tool: Tails comes with a built-in tool for managing VPNs. Navigate to the "Applications" menu, then go to "Internet" and select "Configure Persistent VPN".

Select VPN Service: If you are using a provider like OpenVPN, you will need to configure the VPN with your .ovpn configuration file:

Drag and drop your configuration file into the Tails VPN Configuration Tool.

Follow the prompts to enter your username and password for the VPN service.

Enable VPN: Once you've configured the VPN, select "Start VPN". This will connect you to the VPN server.

Step 2: Verify the VPN Connection in Tails

Check Your IP Address - To verify that the VPN is working, open a terminal and type:

curl ifconfig.me

This should display the IP address of the VPN server rather than your real IP.

Verify the VPN Connection with Tor - After starting the VPN, you can check if Tor is also functioning by visiting the Tor Check page:

torsocks curl https://check.torproject.org

This command will verify that your traffic is being routed through the Tor network.

Step 3: Using the VPN + Tor Combination in Tails

Once the VPN is connected in Tails, your internet traffic will be routed in the following order:

VPN -> Tor -> Internet

This means that your traffic will first pass through the VPN server, hiding your real IP address from your ISP, and then it will be anonymized through the Tor network.

Additional VPN Considerations for Privacy

VPN Provider: It's essential to choose a trustworthy VPN provider with a strong no-logs policy. Popular VPN providers that are known for privacy include ProtonVPN, ExpressVPN, and Mullvad.

Kill Switch: Some VPN services have a kill switch feature that automatically disconnects you from the internet if the VPN connection drops. This is a useful feature to ensure your real IP address is never exposed.

Double VPN Setup: Some VPN providers (such as Mullvad and NordVPN) offer a "Double VPN" feature, where your traffic is routed through two VPN servers, further increasing anonymity.

Chapter 3: Installing and Configuring Tor

What is Tor?

Tor (The Onion Router) is a free, open-source software and network designed to enhance online privacy and anonymity. It allows users to browse the internet without exposing their identity or location by routing their traffic through a decentralized network of volunteer-operated servers, known as "relays" or "nodes."

To access the Dark Web, users must use the Tor browser, which connects to the Tor network and enables anonymous browsing of websites with **.onion** domains.

A deep dive into Tor's architecture and features

At its core, Tor functions by creating an encrypted "onion" structure where each layer of encryption is peeled back at different stages of the route. This decentralized network is made up of a vast array of volunteer-operated relays, each of which only knows its immediate predecessor and successor in the routing chain.

Here's a detailed look at the main components of Tor's architecture:

The Tor Client (Tor Browser)

When a user installs and runs the Tor browser (or uses a Tor-compatible application), the client establishes a connection to the Tor network. The client is responsible for creating the circuits, managing encrypted connections, and performing the necessary steps to ensure data privacy.

The Circuit: Path Through the Tor Network

Once connected, the Tor client randomly selects a path through the network of Tor relays (typically consisting of at least three nodes), which are responsible for forwarding the user's traffic.

The circuit is formed as follows:

Entry Node (Guard Node): The first node in the circuit is called the entry node or guard node. This node knows the user's IP address but does not know the final destination. It only knows that the data will be sent to another Tor node.

Middle Node: The middle node is responsible for relaying the encrypted data between the entry and exit nodes. Importantly, the middle node only knows the previous and next node in the chain and does not have access to either the user's IP address or the final destination of the data.

Exit Node: The final node in the circuit is the exit node. This node decrypts the last layer of encryption and sends the traffic to its final destination on the internet. The exit node can see the data in plaintext if it's not encrypted using protocols like HTTPS, but it cannot identify the original sender of the traffic.

Layers of Encryption: The Onion Layers

The data is encrypted in layers as it travels from the Tor client to the exit node. Each node in the circuit can only decrypt one layer of encryption and then forwards the data to the next node, where the next layer is decrypted. This process is similar to peeling an onion, hence the name "The Onion Router."

Layer 1 (Entry Node): The data is encrypted with the public key of the entry node.

Layer 2 (Middle Node): The middle node decrypts its layer and sends the remaining encrypted data to the next node.

Layer 3 (Exit Node): The exit node decrypts the final layer and forwards the traffic to the destination.

This method ensures that each Tor node only knows about one hop in the chain, providing strong anonymity for the user.

Key Features of Tor

Anonymity and Privacy

Tor provides enhanced privacy by obfuscating the user's location and identity. The multi-hop routing mechanism, combined with encryption, ensures that no single node knows both the sender and the destination. This makes it extremely difficult for adversaries to track the user's activities or correlate their identity with their browsing behavior.

Censorship Circumvention

Because traffic is routed through a global network of volunteer-run nodes, Tor allows users to bypass government censorship and access content that may be blocked in certain regions. Tor can help users access websites that are restricted by firewalls, such as social media platforms or independent news sites.

Onion Services (Hidden Services)

One of Tor's most interesting features is the ability to host anonymous websites, called *onion services* (previously known as *hidden services*). These websites have a special **.onion** domain and can only be accessed through the Tor network.

Onion services provide a higher level of anonymity for both users and website operators. The server hosting an onion service does not reveal its physical location, and communication between the client and the service is encrypted and routed through the Tor network, ensuring that neither party can easily be traced.

Distributed and Decentralized Network

Tor is a decentralized system. Unlike VPN services or proxy servers that rely on a central server, Tor relies on thousands of volunteer-operated relays spread across the globe. This decentralized design minimizes the risk of a single point of failure and reduces the likelihood of surveillance and control by any single entity, such as governments or corporations.

Onion Routing and Resistance to Traffic Analysis

The use of onion routing (multiple layers of encryption and multiple hops through the network) significantly reduces the possibility of traffic analysis by adversaries. If one of the relays is compromised, the attacker can only observe traffic between the compromised node and its adjacent nodes, but not the entire path or the content of the communication.

Privacy for Both Users and Websites

Tor ensures privacy for both the user and the server. While the user's IP address remains anonymous due to the entry and exit node routing, the server hosting an onion service is also protected. These services are hosted on Tor's anonymous **.onion** domain, providing a secure and private method of hosting websites.

Limitations of Tor

Speed and Latency: The Tor network introduces significant latency and can be slow due to the routing of traffic through multiple relays. This is especially noticeable for activities like streaming or large downloads.

Exit Node Vulnerabilities: While the entry and middle nodes provide robust privacy protections, the exit node has the ability to decrypt the final layer of encryption and view the unencrypted data being transmitted. If the traffic is not encrypted with HTTPS or another protocol, an exit node could potentially spy on the data.

Misuse of the Network: Tor is often associated with the "dark web," which contains both legal and illegal activities. While Tor itself is not illegal, some users exploit its anonymity to engage in illegal activities, such as trafficking, fraud, or hacking.

False Sense of Security: While Tor provides strong privacy protection, it is not a catch-all solution. For instance, Tor does not protect against malware, and users must also be cautious about revealing personal information in their online interactions.

Installing Tor on Linux

Installing Tor on Linux is a straightforward process that can be done through the package manager for your distribution. For most Linux distributions, you can install Tor by first adding the official Tor Project repository to your system's software sources. On Ubuntu and Debian-based systems, you can use the following commands to update your package list, install Tor, and start the Tor service: sudo apt update, sudo apt install tor, and sudo systemctl start tor. For Fedora, use sudo dnf install tor. Once installed, Tor can be configured by editing its configuration file, typically located at /etc/tor/torrc. After installation, you can also install the Tor Browser to access the Tor network for anonymous browsing, or use Tor through other applications by configuring them to use Tor as a proxy.

Step-by-step guide for installation (with code examples)

Installing Tor on Debian/Ubuntu

Step 1: Add the Tor Project's Repository

To ensure you're installing the latest version of Tor, you'll need to add the official Tor Project repository.

First, open a terminal window and update your system's package list:

sudo apt update

Install the necessary packages to fetch the Tor repository:

sudo apt install apt-transport-https curl

Next, download and add the Tor Project's GPG key:

curl https://www.torproject.org/static/tor-archive-key.asc | sudo tee /etc/apt/trusted.gpg.d/tor.asc

Add the Tor repository to your system:

sudo nano /etc/apt/sources.list.d/tor.list

Add the following line (for Debian/Ubuntu systems):

deb https://deb.torproject.org/torproject.org stretch main

Press Ctrl+X, then Y, and finally Enter to save and exit.

Step 2: Update the Package List

After adding the Tor repository, update the package list to include Tor's latest package:

sudo apt update

Step 3: Install Tor

Now, install Tor using the apt package manager:

sudo apt install tor

Step 4: Enable and Start the Tor Service

After installation, you can enable and start the Tor service:

sudo systemctl enable tor

sudo systemctl start tor

Step 5: Verify the Tor Service

To ensure that Tor is running correctly, check its status:

sudo systemctl status tor

If the service is running properly, you should see an active status.

Step 6: Install the Tor Browser (Optional)

To access the Tor network through the browser, install the Tor Browser.

The easiest way is to download it from the official Tor Browser download page or use the command line:

sudo apt install torbrowser-launcher

Then, launch the Tor Browser:

torbrowser-launcher

Installing Tor on Tails

Tails is a live Linux distribution focused on privacy and anonymity, and Tor is pre-installed on it. However, if you need to update or reconfigure it, here's how you can do it.

Step 1: Boot into Tails: Start your Tails USB stick or DVD and boot into the live environment.

Step 2: Open the Applications Menu: Once Tails is booted up, Tor is already running. You can check its status by opening a terminal and typing:

systemctl status tor

Step 3: Verify Tor's Connection

You can verify that Tor is running and properly connected to the Tor network by visiting a Tor-specific website, such as:

https://check.torproject.org/

This website will tell you if you are using Tor and if your connection is secure.

Step 4: Start Using Tor Browser (Pre-installed)

Tails comes with the Tor Browser pre-installed, so you can start using it right away:

Open the Applications menu.

Go to Internet and click on Tor Browser.

Follow the instructions to connect to the Tor network and begin anonymous browsing.

Verifying the installation and basic configurations

Once you have installed Tor on your Linux system (whether on Debian/Ubuntu or Tails), it's crucial to verify that Tor is running correctly and properly configured. Below are steps to check that Tor is functioning as expected and how to troubleshoot basic configurations.

Verifying Tor Installation on Debian/Ubuntu

Step 1: Check if Tor is Running

After installing Tor, it should automatically start as a service.

To verify that it's running, you can use the following command to check the status of the Tor service:

sudo systemctl status tor

You should see an output indicating that Tor is active and running, something like:

tor.service - Tor service

   Loaded: loaded (/lib/systemd/system/tor.service; enabled; vendor preset: enabled)

   Active: active (running) since [date and time]

If Tor isn't running, start it with:

sudo systemctl start tor

Step 2: Verify Tor's Connectivity

Once the service is running, verify that your Tor connection is working.

You can check the status of your connection to the Tor network by visiting the following URL in a web browser that routes through Tor (like the Tor Browser or any application configured to use Tor):

https://check.torproject.org/

This website will confirm whether you are connected to the Tor network. If you see a message that says **"Congratulations. This browser is configured to use Tor."**, then everything is set up correctly.

Alternatively, you can use the command-line tool curl to check your IP address through the Tor network:

curl https://check.torproject.org/api/ip

If your IP address is different from your real IP address, Tor is successfully anonymizing your traffic.

Step 3: Checking Tor Logs for Errors If you encounter issues, Tor's logs can provide helpful information. You can check the logs by viewing the Tor service's log output:

journalctl -u tor

Look for any errors or warnings that may indicate misconfigurations or connection issues.

Verifying Tor Installation on Tails

On Tails, Tor is pre-installed and running by default.

Here's how to verify its status:

Step 1: Verify Tor's Connection

Since Tails uses Tor automatically to protect your anonymity, the easiest way to verify if it's working is to visit the Check Tor Project website:

https://check.torproject.org/

If the page displays **"Congratulations. This browser is configured to use Tor."**, your Tor connection is active.

Step 2: Check Tor's Status from the Terminal

To confirm that the Tor service is running, open a terminal and check the service status:

systemctl status tor

You should see something like:

tor.service - Anonymizing Overlay Network

   Loaded: loaded (/lib/systemd/system/tor.service; enabled; vendor preset: enabled)

   Active: active (running) since [date and time]

If Tor isn't running for some reason, try restarting it with:

sudo systemctl restart tor

Step 3: Verify the Tor Browser

Tails also includes the Tor Browser, which is pre-configured to work with Tor. You can launch it from the Applications menu under Internet > Tor Browser. Once opened, it will automatically connect to the Tor network and allow anonymous browsing.

Basic Tor Configuration (Debian/Ubuntu and Tails)

While Tor is ready to use after installation, you may want to modify its default settings for performance or privacy reasons. Here are some common configurations:

Step 1: Edit the Tor Configuration File

Tor's configuration file is located at /etc/tor/torrc on Debian/Ubuntu systems. This file controls various aspects of Tor's behavior.

To edit it, open it with a text editor (e.g., nano):

sudo nano /etc/tor/torrc

Here are some basic configurations you might want to change:

Set a specific exit node (if you want to use a specific country's Tor exit node):

ExitNodes {us}

Disable DNS resolution via Tor for specific applications:

DNSPort 9053

Configure a hidden service (useful for setting up your own .onion site):

HiddenServiceDir /var/lib/tor/hidden_service/

HiddenServicePort 80 127.0.0.1:80

Once you've made the desired changes, save the file and restart the Tor service to apply the changes:

sudo systemctl restart tor

Step 2: Configure Tor to Start Automatically

To make sure that Tor starts automatically when the system boots up, run:

sudo systemctl enable tor

Step 3: Using Tor for Specific Applications

To route specific applications (such as a web browser or email client) through Tor, you'll need to configure those applications to use Tor's SOCKS proxy. By default, Tor listens on port 9050 for SOCKS connections.

For example, you can configure Firefox to use Tor by setting the SOCKS proxy settings to:

SOCKS Host: 127.0.0.1

SOCKS Port: 9050

Running a Tor Service

Running a Tor service involves setting up and configuring Tor to anonymize traffic and potentially host a **.onion** site through the Tor network. To start a Tor service, you must install and configure the Tor software on your server, ensuring it's set to run as a background service that automatically starts on boot. The Tor service can be configured via the torrc file, where you can specify settings like hidden services, exit node preferences, and other privacy configurations. Once the service is running, you can verify it's functioning by checking the Tor logs, using the systemctl command to monitor its status, and ensuring that your service is correctly routing traffic. For hosting a **.onion** site, you need to define a hidden service directory and map local ports to external ones, allowing your website to be accessed anonymously via the Tor network.

Setting up a private Tor relay (optional)

Setting up a private Tor relay is an optional but effective way to contribute to the Tor network and enhance its anonymity and performance. A private relay helps route traffic through the Tor network, improving its overall security and decentralization. To set up a private Tor relay, you first need to install Tor on a dedicated machine or server. After installation, you configure the Tor relay by editing the torrc file, which is typically located at /etc/tor/torrc on Linux systems. In the torrc file, you can specify the relay's type— either a guard (entry node), middle (relay), or exit node, depending on the role you wish your relay to play. You'll also want to assign a unique nickname to your relay, and optionally configure bandwidth limits and other parameters. Once set up, you can start the Tor service and verify its status through the Tor logs. It's essential to ensure that your relay is properly secured, with firewall rules restricting access and a reliable, high-speed internet connection to handle traffic. While running a relay can improve the performance and resilience of the Tor network, it's important to be aware of potential legal and security considerations, especially when running an exit node, as exit traffic is the final point before reaching the destination on the open internet.

Step-by-Step Guide to Setting Up a Private Tor Relay

Install Tor

Start by installing the Tor package on your server.

On Debian/Ubuntu systems, use the following commands:

sudo apt update

sudo apt install tor

Configure the Tor Relay

Once Tor is installed, you need to configure the relay by editing the torrc file. Open the file with a text editor:

sudo nano /etc/tor/torrc

Add or modify the following lines to configure the Tor relay:

Set a nickname for your relay
Nickname MyPrivateRelay

Set the relay type (you can choose Guard, Middle, or Exit)
RelayBandwidthRate 100 KB # Bandwidth limits (optional)
RelayBandwidthBurst 200 KB # Maximum bandwidth burst (optional)

Set a contact email address (recommended)
ContactInfo your-email@example.com

Set the IP address or domain to listen for incoming traffic
ORPort 9001 # Listening port for Tor relay

Optionally, if you want to make it an Exit relay, use this:
ExitPolicy accept *:80, accept *:443, reject *:* # Allows HTTP and HTTPS traffic only

Enable the relay to be advertised in the Tor network

DirPort 9030 # Port used for directory traffic (optional)

Optional: Set bandwidth limits for your relay
These limits control how much bandwidth your relay will use and allow others to use through it.
Note: Be cautious with these limits as they directly affect your server's bandwidth.

Explanation of key settings:

Nickname: This is the unique name for your relay that will be used to identify it in the Tor network.

RelayBandwidthRate and **RelayBandwidthBurst**: These settings control how much bandwidth your relay can use. You can adjust them based on your server's capabilities.

ExitPolicy: If you want your relay to be an **Exit Node**, you can specify which ports it should allow (e.g., HTTP, HTTPS). If you want to limit this to just relaying traffic within the Tor network, you can leave this option out or set it to restrict exit traffic.

ContactInfo: This is recommended to provide a contact email for network administrators to reach you if necessary.

Restart the Tor Service

After saving the changes to the torrc file, restart the Tor service to apply the configuration:

sudo systemctl restart tor

Verify the Relay Is Running

To check if your Tor relay is running properly, you can check the status of the Tor service:

sudo systemctl status tor

Additionally, you can inspect the Tor logs to verify that your relay is being advertised and functioning correctly:

tail -f /var/log/tor/log

Look for lines that confirm your relay is active and connected to the Tor network.

Verify Your Relay's Status

Once the relay is running, you can check its status in the Tor network by visiting the Tor Metrics website. Enter your relay's nickname to see its status, performance, and how much traffic it's handling.

Alternatively, you can use the Tor Network Status page to ensure your relay is part of the network:

https://onionoo.torproject.org/

Optional: Set Bandwidth Limits

If you want to limit the bandwidth of your relay, you can adjust the RelayBandwidthRate and RelayBandwidthBurst settings in the torrc file as needed.

For example, to set your relay to use a maximum of 1 MB/s of bandwidth:

RelayBandwidthRate 1024 KB

RelayBandwidthBurst 2048 KB

Important Notes:

Security: Ensure that your server is secured and has appropriate firewall rules. By default, Tor relays are open to the internet, but you should consider restricting access to specific IP addresses if you don't want random users to connect.

Exit Node Considerations: Running a Exit Node means that your server will route traffic from the Tor network to the open internet. Be cautious, as exit nodes can be legally sensitive, depending on the traffic being routed through them.

Bandwidth: The more bandwidth you allocate to your relay, the more traffic your server will handle. Make sure your server's internet connection can handle the load without affecting its performance.

Monitoring and managing Tor services

Monitoring and managing your Tor services is crucial for ensuring optimal performance, security, and reliability, especially if you are running a private relay or hosting a **.onion** site. Several tools and methods are available to help you track the health and performance of your Tor services, identify potential issues, and make adjustments when necessary.

Checking the Status of Tor

One of the first steps in managing a Tor service is regularly checking its status to ensure it is running smoothly. You can use the following system commands to check the Tor service:

Systemd Status (for most Linux distributions):

sudo systemctl status tor

This command provides a summary of the Tor service, including whether it's active and running. If there's an issue with Tor, this command will show you any errors or problems.

Log Monitoring:

You can also monitor Tor's log files to troubleshoot and see the real-time operation of the service:

tail -f /var/log/tor/log

This command will display the latest log entries from Tor. The logs can provide important information about the state of your Tor relay, including connection issues, any errors related to your **.onion** site, or bandwidth usage.

Monitoring Tor Traffic and Performance

Tor provides built-in metrics to track the performance of your relay. You can use Tor Metrics or look at the log files for more details about traffic flow:

Tor Metrics Website: Visit Tor Metrics to monitor real-time statistics of your relay, including its uptime, bandwidth usage, and relay health. By entering your relay's nickname or fingerprint, you can see how well your relay is contributing to the network and whether it's effectively routing traffic.

Bandwidth Usage: In your torrc configuration file, you can set limits for your relay's bandwidth, which can be useful to prevent overloading your server. To manage bandwidth usage, regularly check the RelayBandwidthRate and

RelayBandwidthBurst settings. Additionally, monitoring external tools like vnstat or iftop can help assess overall network traffic.

Setting Up Alerts for Tor Services

For more advanced management, you can set up monitoring and alerting systems to notify you when there are issues with your Tor service. Using tools like Monit or Nagios, you can automate alerts for Tor service failures, restarts, or performance bottlenecks.

Monit Example - To use Monit to monitor the Tor service, install it with:

sudo apt install monit

Then, configure Monit to check the status of the Tor process by editing the Monit configuration file (/etc/monit/monitrc):

check process tor with pidfile /var/run/tor/tor.pid

  start program = "/etc/init.d/tor start"

  stop program = "/etc/init.d/tor stop"

  if failed port 9050 then restart

This example ensures Monit checks if Tor is running on port 9050 and restarts it if the service is down.

Managing Tor Configuration Changes

To modify the configuration of your Tor relay or hidden service, you can edit the torrc file located at /etc/tor/torrc.

After making any changes, restart the Tor service for the new settings to take effect:

sudo systemctl restart tor

For hidden services, ensure you update the HiddenServiceDir and HiddenServicePort directives if necessary to change the configuration of your **.onion** site. Always check for proper permissions on the HiddenServiceDir directory to ensure Tor can write and manage its private keys.

Troubleshooting Tor Services

If your Tor service is experiencing issues, there are several common troubleshooting steps:

Verify Configurations: Double-check your torrc file for syntax errors or misconfigurations.

Check Log Files: Use tail -f /var/log/tor/log to see if there are specific errors in the log files related to connectivity, traffic handling, or service crashes.

Check Tor Network Status: Sometimes, your relay might not be able to connect to the Tor network due to issues with upstream providers or Tor's internal network. Use the

Tor Network Status page to verify if there are any network-wide issues.

Firewall Configuration: Ensure that your server's firewall allows traffic on the relevant Tor ports (e.g., ORPort for relays or DirPort for directory services).

Exit Node Issues: If you're running an exit node, make sure your ExitPolicy is correctly configured. Misconfiguration can result in the Tor network marking your relay as misbehaving.

Scaling and Updating Tor Services

As your Tor service grows, you may need to adjust the configuration to handle more traffic or add more bandwidth. Scaling up could involve increasing the RelayBandwidthRate or adding more relays to handle larger volumes of traffic.

Also, ensure that you regularly update your Tor installation to stay protected against security vulnerabilities by running:

sudo apt update

sudo apt upgrade tor

Regular updates are crucial as Tor continuously releases security patches and new features to enhance the privacy and stability of its network.

Chapter 4: Setting Up an Onion Site

Understanding Onion Domains (.onion)

Onion domains, or **.onion** addresses, are special top-level domains used exclusively within the Tor network. These domains are part of the dark web, a subset of the internet that is not indexed by traditional search engines and requires specialized software like the Tor Browser to access. Unlike standard domain names, which are linked to IP addresses, **.onion** addresses are derived from cryptographic keys, providing enhanced anonymity and security. A **.onion** address typically appears as a long, random string of characters followed by the ".**onion**" suffix (e.g., 3g2upl4pq6kufc4m.onion). This unique structure ensures that the website's server is not easily traceable, offering a layer of privacy for both website owners and users. Because of this, **.onion** domains are often used for privacy-focused services, secure communications, or for hosting websites that need to maintain a high level of anonymity.

How to generate a .onion address

Generating a **.onion** address involves setting up a Tor hidden service, which allows you to create an anonymous and secure website accessible only through the Tor network. The process relies on the cryptographic features built into Tor, which automatically generates a unique **.onion** address for your service.

Here's how to generate a .onion address:

To generate a **.onion** address, you first need to have Tor installed on your system. This is usually done by installing the Tor package from your distribution's repository.

For example, on Debian/Ubuntu:

sudo apt update

sudo apt install tor

Once installed, ensure Tor is running on your system:

sudo systemctl start tor

sudo systemctl enable tor

Configure the Hidden Service

To create a **.onion** address, you need to configure Tor to create a hidden service. This is done by editing the Tor configuration file (torrc), typically located in /etc/tor/torrc on Linux systems.

Open the file in a text editor:

sudo nano /etc/tor/torrc

Add the following lines to the file to specify the directory where the hidden service files will be stored and the port it will run on:

HiddenServiceDir /var/lib/tor/hidden_service/

HiddenServicePort 80 127.0.0.1:80

HiddenServiceDir specifies the directory where Tor will store the keys and configuration for your hidden service.

HiddenServicePort maps the port (e.g., 80) on your **.onion** address to the corresponding port on your local server (e.g., 127.0.0.1:80).

Restart Tor

After saving your changes to the torrc file, restart Tor to apply the new configuration:

sudo systemctl restart tor

Locate the .onion Address

Once Tor restarts, it will automatically generate a **.onion** address for your hidden service. You can find this address in the HiddenServiceDir directory you specified earlier. By default, the hostname file inside this directory contains the generated **.onion** address.

For example:

cat /var/lib/tor/hidden_service/hostname

This command will output a string like:

3g2upl4pq6kufc4m.onion

This is your unique **.onion** address. It is a cryptographic hash generated by Tor, ensuring anonymity for both the service and its users.

Access Your .onion Address

Now, your **.onion** address is active, and you can access it through the Tor Browser. Simply type the generated address into the Tor Browser's address bar, and you'll be directed to your hidden service.

Additional Considerations

Security: Ensure your hidden service is properly secured, as your **.onion** address can still be vulnerable if the underlying web server or application is not configured securely.

Service Ports: You can specify other ports for different services by adding additional HiddenServicePort lines in the torrc file (e.g., for SSH, email, etc.).

Introduction to Tor hidden services

Tor hidden services are a unique feature of the Tor network that allow individuals and organizations to host websites, services, or applications in a completely anonymous and secure manner. Unlike traditional websites, which are hosted on the surface web and are accessible via regular domain names (such as .com or .org), Tor hidden services operate within the Tor network, using special **.onion** domain names. These services are designed to ensure privacy for both the server hosting the service and the users accessing it.

A Tor hidden service can be anything from a simple website to a secure email server or a messaging platform. The key advantage of a hidden service is that it doesn't expose the server's real IP address to the public internet. Instead, the **.onion** address and associated cryptographic keys are the only identifiers that point to the service, effectively hiding the server's physical location and identity. This makes it extremely difficult for anyone to trace the server back to its real-world location, offering enhanced security for both the owner and visitors.

How Tor Hidden Services Work

Tor hidden services rely on the decentralized, privacy-preserving infrastructure of the Tor network. When a user accesses a hidden service, their connection is routed through multiple nodes (relays) in the Tor network, which anonymizes their traffic. The service itself also communicates through Tor's onion routing, ensuring that the origin of the server remains hidden from any external observer.

Tor's hidden service architecture uses a two-layer encryption system:

Hidden Service Descriptor: The hidden service first generates a descriptor that includes its public key and information about its Tor location (the entry node and hidden service address). This descriptor is then uploaded to a special Tor directory.

Encrypted Communication: When a user tries to connect to a hidden service, Tor retrieves the service's descriptor and establishes an encrypted communication path between the client and the hidden service, ensuring that no intermediary can trace the traffic.

Advantages of Tor Hidden Services

Anonymity and Privacy: Both the server and the client are anonymized, with neither party's real IP address being exposed to the other. This makes hidden services ideal for use in environments where privacy is paramount, such as for journalists, whistleblowers, or privacy-conscious individuals.

Censorship Resistance: Since Tor hidden services are part of the decentralized Tor network, they are resistant to government censorship and IP-based blocking. This makes it harder for authorities to shut down or block access to a hidden service based on geographic location.

Security: The use of **.onion** addresses and encryption ensures that communications between users and hidden services are secure from surveillance and attacks. Tor's multi-layer encryption and decentralized nature make it

more resistant to cyberattacks like DDoS or surveillance.

Setting Up a Web Server for Onion Sites

Setting up a web server for onion sites involves configuring a server to host websites accessible only via the Tor network. Onion sites, also known as hidden services, provide anonymity for both the server and users by routing traffic through Tor's decentralized network, masking IP addresses. To create a web server for onion sites, you'll need to install a Tor service on a Linux server, generate a unique **.onion** address, and configure a web server like Apache or Nginx to handle incoming Tor connections. It's essential to ensure robust security measures, such as using HTTPS with self-signed certificates and applying server hardening techniques, to protect the hidden service from potential vulnerabilities while maintaining user privacy.

Installing and configuring Apache or Nginx on Linux

Installing and configuring Apache or Nginx on a Linux server is a straightforward process that allows you to host web content, whether using HTTP or HTTPS. Below are step-by-step instructions for setting up both HTTP and HTTPS on Apache and Nginx.

For onion sites, SSL is not strictly required because the Tor network itself already provides end-to-end encryption between the user and the server. This encryption ensures that both the server's location and the user's identity remain anonymous and secure. However, many administrators still choose to use SSL for added layers of encryption and to maintain best security practices. Using SSL on an onion site can help protect data from being tampered with between the Tor network and the application layer, enhance the site's credibility, and allow for easier integration with existing tools that expect HTTPS traffic. In general, while SSL is not necessary for the functioning of an onion site, it can provide additional security and is often used to complement the Tor network's encryption.

For Apache (HTTP):

Update your package manager:
On Ubuntu/Debian: sudo apt update

On CentOS/RHEL: sudo yum update

Install Apache:

On Ubuntu/Debian: sudo apt install apache2

On CentOS/RHEL: sudo yum install httpd

Start and enable Apache service:

On Ubuntu/Debian:

sudo systemctl start apache2 && sudo systemctl enable apache2

On CentOS/RHEL:

sudo systemctl start httpd && sudo systemctl enable httpd

Configure Apache:

Apache configuration files are located in /etc/apache2/ (Ubuntu/Debian) or /etc/httpd/ (CentOS/RHEL). You can modify files such as apache2.conf or httpd.conf to customize settings like virtual hosts, directory permissions, etc.

Firewall Configuration: Ensure that port 80 (HTTP) is open for incoming connections.

Ubuntu/Debian:

sudo ufw allow 'Apache Full'

CentOS/RHEL:

```
sudo firewall-cmd --add-service=http --permanent && sudo
firewall-cmd –reload
```

For Apache (HTTPS):

Install OpenSSL:

On Ubuntu/Debian:

```
sudo apt install openssl
```

On CentOS/RHEL:

```
sudo yum install mod_ssl
```

Enable SSL module and configure SSL settings:

Ubuntu/Debian:

```
sudo a2enmod ssl
```

Create or modify your SSL virtual host configuration file in /etc/apache2/sites-available/ (e.g., default-ssl.conf).

Obtain an SSL certificate:

You can get a free SSL certificate from Let's Encrypt using tools like Certbot:

Install Certbot:

```
sudo apt install certbot python3-certbot-apache
```

Obtain the certificate:

sudo certbot --apache

Open HTTPS firewall port:

On Ubuntu/Debian:

sudo ufw allow 'Apache Secure'

On CentOS/RHEL:

sudo firewall-cmd --add-service=https --permanent && sudo firewall-cmd --reload

Restart Apache:

sudo systemctl restart apache2 or sudo systemctl restart httpd.

For Nginx (HTTP):

Update your package manager:

On Ubuntu/Debian:

sudo apt update

On CentOS/RHEL:

sudo yum update

Install Nginx:

On Ubuntu/Debian:

sudo apt install nginx

On CentOS/RHEL:

sudo yum install nginx

Start and enable Nginx service:

sudo systemctl start nginx && sudo systemctl enable nginx

Configure Nginx:

Nginx configuration files are located in /etc/nginx/. You can modify nginx.conf or create site-specific configuration files in /etc/nginx/sites-available/ and link them to /etc/nginx/sites-enabled/.

Firewall Configuration: Ensure that port 80 (HTTP) is open for incoming connections.

Ubuntu/Debian:

sudo ufw allow 'Nginx HTTP'

CentOS/RHEL:

sudo firewall-cmd --add-service=http --permanent && sudo firewall-cmd --reload

For Nginx (HTTPS):

Install OpenSSL:

On Ubuntu/Debian:

sudo apt install openssl

On CentOS/RHEL:

sudo yum install openssl

Obtain an SSL certificate:

Use Certbot to get a free SSL certificate:

Install Certbot:

sudo apt install certbot python3-certbot-nginx

Obtain the certificate:

sudo certbot --nginx

Configure Nginx for SSL:

Update your server block in /etc/nginx/sites-available/ to listen on port 443 and include SSL certificates.

Open HTTPS firewall port:

On Ubuntu/Debian:

sudo ufw allow 'Nginx HTTPS'

On CentOS/RHEL:

sudo firewall-cmd --add-service=https --permanent && sudo firewall-cmd --reload

Restart Nginx:

sudo systemctl restart nginx.

Note on SSL:

While SSL is not strictly required for basic HTTP functionality, it is highly recommended to secure your site with HTTPS, especially for sensitive data or user interactions. SSL encrypts the connection between the server and the client, providing enhanced security and trust.

Ensuring privacy and security for your web server

Ensuring privacy and security for your web server on the dark web is critical to protect both your data and users, as the dark web is frequented by many hackers. One key step in enhancing security is to avoid using default directory locations like /var/www for hosting your website, as these are common targets for attackers. Instead, you can place your web files in a different directory, such as $USER/public_html, which makes it harder for potential attackers to locate. This simple change adds an extra layer of security by obscuring the default file structure that many automated hacking tools are designed to exploit.

In addition to this, keeping your server software up to date is crucial since security patches are regularly released to address vulnerabilities. Using strong, unique passwords, or better yet, SSH key-based authentication for accessing your server can further protect your system. You should also configure a firewall to only allow necessary ports, such as HTTP/HTTPS (ports 80/443), reducing exposure to attacks.

Using HTTPS with an SSL certificate ensures that communication between the server and users is encrypted, safeguarding sensitive information. Hardening your server by disabling unused modules, enforcing secure headers like Content Security Policy (CSP) and HTTP Strict Transport Security (HSTS), and properly setting file permissions further decreases the risk of breaches. Monitoring server logs for unusual activity and using intrusion detection systems (IDS) will help identify unauthorized access attempts. Regularly backing up your data in a secure manner provides additional protection against data loss or ransomware. By implementing these practices, you can significantly enhance the privacy and security of your web server.

Example: Moving Website Directory and Enhancing Security

Create a new directory for your website

Instead of using the default /var/www, create a new directory within your user's home directory.

For example, if your username is myuser, you can create a directory like /home/myuser/public_html:

mkdir -p /home/myuser/public_html

Move your website files:

Move your website files from their default location which is /var/www/html to your new directory /home/myuser/public_html:

mv /var/www/html/* /home/myuser/public_html/

Update the web server configuration:

For Apache, edit the configuration file (commonly found in /etc/apache2/sites-available/000-default.conf or /etc/httpd/conf/httpd.conf):

sudo nano /etc/apache2/sites-available/000-default.conf

Change the DocumentRoot directive to point to the new location:

DocumentRoot /home/myuser/public_html

For Nginx, update the configuration file (commonly found in /etc/nginx/sites-available/default or /etc/nginx/nginx.conf):

sudo nano /etc/nginx/sites-available/default

Modify the root directive:

nginx

root /home/myuser/public_html;

Set appropriate permissions: Ensure the web server (Apache or Nginx) has the necessary permissions to access the new directory.

You can do this by adjusting ownership:

sudo chown -R www-data:www-data /home/myuser/public_html

Also, ensure that the directory has proper read and execute permissions for the web server:

sudo chmod -R 755 /home/myuser/public_html

Restart the web server: After making these changes, restart your web server to apply the configuration.

For Apache:

sudo systemctl restart apache2

For Nginx:

sudo systemctl restart nginx

Additional Security Enhancements:

SSL (HTTPS): Ensure secure communication by using SSL certificates. You can obtain free SSL certificates from Let's Encrypt and configure Apache or Nginx to use HTTPS by editing the virtual host files and pointing them to your SSL certificates.

Example for Apache:

```
<VirtualHost *:443>
    DocumentRoot /home/myuser/public_html
    SSLEngine on
    SSLCertificateFile /etc/ssl/certs/yourcert.pem
    SSLCertificateKeyFile /etc/ssl/private/yourkey.pem
</VirtualHost>
```

Example for Nginx:

```
server {
    listen 443 ssl;
    root /home/myuser/public_html;
    ssl_certificate /etc/ssl/certs/yourcert.pem;
    ssl_certificate_key /etc/ssl/private/yourkey.pem;
}
```

Firewall Setup: Limit server exposure by configuring a firewall to only allow essential traffic.

For example, use ufw to allow only HTTP (80) and HTTPS (443):

```
sudo ufw allow 80/tcp
sudo ufw allow 443/tcp
sudo ufw enable
```

Harden Web Server Configuration: Disable unused modules, and ensure headers like X-Content-Type-Options and Strict-Transport-Security are set to secure the server.

For example, in Apache:

```
Header set X-Content-Type-Options "nosniff"
```

Header always set Strict-Transport-Security "max-age=31536000; includeSubDomains"

By moving your web files to a non-default directory and

following these best practices, you make it harder for attackers to locate and target your files while ensuring secure communication and limiting attack surfaces.

Configuring your web server to run on Tor

Configuring your web server to run on Tor involves setting up your server to be accessible via the Tor network, which allows users to access your site anonymously through a **.onion** address. This process enhances privacy and security for both the server and its users by hiding the server's real IP address and location.

If you haven't already, install Tor on Your Server

First, you need to install the Tor software on your web server.

On a Debian-based system like Ubuntu, you can install Tor using the following commands:

sudo apt update

sudo apt install tor

For Red Hat-based systems, use:

sudo yum install tor

Configure Tor for Hidden Services

Once Tor is installed, you need to configure it to run a hidden service (i.e., your website on the .onion network). Edit the Tor configuration file located at /etc/tor/torrc:

sudo nano /etc/tor/torrc

Add the following lines to the end of the file to specify the port your web server will run on (e.g., port 80 for HTTP or 443 for HTTPS) and where Tor should forward the traffic:

HiddenServiceDir /var/lib/tor/hidden_service/

HiddenServicePort 80 127.0.0.1:80

In this example, HiddenServiceDir specifies the directory where Tor will store the hidden service keys, and HiddenServicePort tells Tor to forward incoming traffic on port 80 (HTTP) to your web server running on 127.0.0.1:80.

Restart Tor to Apply the Changes

After saving your changes, restart the Tor service to apply the new configuration:

sudo systemctl restart tor

Find Your .onion Address

Once Tor restarts, it will generate your **.onion** address.

You can find this address by navigating to the directory you specified for the hidden service (/var/lib/tor/hidden_service/) and looking for the hostname file:

sudo cat /var/lib/tor/hidden_service/hostname

This file contains your **.onion** address, which can be used to access your website on the Tor network.

Configure Your Web Server

Now that Tor is set up to forward traffic to your web server, ensure your web server (Apache, Nginx, etc.) is configured to listen on the correct local port (127.0.0.1).

For example, if you're using Apache, ensure your virtual host is configured to listen only on 127.0.0.1:

```
<VirtualHost 127.0.0.1:80>

    DocumentRoot /home/myuser/public_html

    ServerName youronionaddress.onion

    # Other configuration settings

</VirtualHost>
```

Similarly, configure Nginx to listen on the local interface:

```
server {

    listen 127.0.0.1:80;

    server_name youronionaddress.onion;

    root /home/myuser/public_html;

    # Other configuration settings

}
```

Testing Your Tor Site

Once the configuration is complete, you can test your **.onion** site by using the Tor browser. Open the Tor browser and navigate to your **.onion** address, such as http://youronionaddress.onion. Your website should be accessible through Tor.

Enhancing Security (Optional)

SSL/TLS on .onion: While Tor already provides encryption between the user and the server, you can still configure SSL/TLS on your server to ensure that communication between Tor and your web server is secure.

Firewall Configuration: It's a good idea to restrict your web server to listen only on the local loopback address (127.0.0.1) to prevent direct access from the public internet.

Obfuscation: If desired, you can configure additional layers of obfuscation for your **.onion** address using features like "hidden service v3 addresses" or using multiple Tor nodes for additional privacy.

Creating and Deploying Your Onion Site

Creating and deploying any website as an onion site involves configuring your existing website to be accessible through the Tor network, ensuring anonymity and security for both the server and its users. The process begins by installing and configuring a web server, such as Apache or Nginx, to host the website as you normally would for a standard HTTP/HTTPS site. The key difference is that you then set up a hidden service in Tor, which routes traffic through the Tor network, creating a unique **.onion** address. Once Tor is configured to forward requests to your web server, your website will be accessible solely through Tor, ensuring that users can browse your site anonymously. This allows any website, whether it's a basic informational page or a more complex service, to be deployed on the Tor network with the added benefit of privacy and security.

Creating a basic HTML page as your onion site

Creating a basic HTML page as your onion site is a simple and effective way to get started with hosting on the Tor network. The first step is to set up your web server (Apache or Nginx) to serve web content locally, as mentioned in the process of configuring a Tor hidden service. Once Tor is installed and configured to forward traffic to your web server, you can deploy a basic HTML page.

Example:

Create the HTML Page: Create a simple HTML file to serve as your onion site's content.

For example, create a file named index.html:

```
<!DOCTYPE html>
<html lang="en">
<head>
  <meta charset="UTF-8">
  <meta name="viewport" content="width=device-width, initial-scale=1.0">
  <title>Welcome to My Onion Site</title>
</head>
```

```
<body>

    <h1>Welcome to My Onion Site!</h1>

    <p>This website is hosted on the Tor network for enhanced
privacy.</p>

</body>

</html>
```

Place the HTML File: Place the index.html file in the web server's root directory, typically located in $USER/public_html or /var/www/html, depending on your configuration.

Configure Tor Hidden Service - In the Tor configuration file (/etc/tor/torrc), add the hidden service configuration:

HiddenServiceDir /var/lib/tor/hidden_service/

HiddenServicePort 80 127.0.0.1:80

This tells Tor to route incoming traffic for your **.onion** address to the web server running on port 80 locally.

Restart Tor - Restart the Tor service to apply the changes:

sudo systemctl restart tor

Access Your .onion Site: Once Tor restarts, it generates a unique **.onion** address for your site.

You can find the address by checking the hostname file in /var/lib/tor/hidden_service/:

sudo cat /var/lib/tor/hidden_service/hostname

Open the Tor browser and navigate to the **.onion** address provided to access your basic HTML page anonymously.

Making your .onion site visible on the Tor network search engines

Adding your onion site address to search engines on the Tor network is a different process than submitting to traditional search engines like Google. While Google indexes and ranks websites through its centralized system of crawling, the Tor network operates in a decentralized and anonymous manner, meaning that any indexing service for **.onion** sites is unique and tailored to the Tor environment.

How It Works on the Tor Network:

Search Engines for the Dark Web: Unlike Google, which indexes content from the surface web (clearly accessible via regular browsers), search engines on the Tor network index **.onion** websites. Some popular search engines on Tor include DuckDuckGo (on Tor), Ahmia, and NotEvil, which specifically crawl the **.onion** domain space and help users discover hidden services.

Privacy and Anonymity: When adding your **.onion** address to a Tor search engine, the process is handled with privacy in mind. Unlike Google, where your website is often linked to identifiable information and tracked across different sources, the search engines for the Tor network generally don't track users or store personal data. However, you still need to be cautious because some Tor search engines may compromise your privacy or could potentially expose your site to unwanted traffic or scrutiny if not carefully selected.

Careful Listing: Before submitting your onion address to any search engine, it's important to choose services that are known for upholding privacy and security standards. Some search engines on Tor might track IPs or have weak security, which could potentially expose your site to the wrong audience. Always verify that the search engine has a strong reputation within the Tor community and does not log user activity or expose search results in an unsecured way.

Indexing Process: When your onion site is indexed, the search engine crawls your site via the Tor network, indexing its content anonymously. The site will then appear in search results, accessible only to users with the Tor browser. However, unlike Google, where your site could be indexed quickly and appear on the first page for specific keywords, search results on Tor are often more limited and specialized due to the niche nature of **.onion** domains.

Be Cautious with Who You List With: It's essential to be cautious when choosing where to list your onion address. Some Tor search engines may be set up to track the popularity of certain sites or use information for purposes outside of maintaining privacy. Avoid adding your site to platforms or services that might jeopardize your anonymity or compromise the security of your website. Research and choose only reputable, privacy-focused search engines that cater specifically to the Tor community.

Adding your onion site to search engines within the Tor network differs from the traditional approach of submitting to Google. While Tor search engines index **.onion** sites for anonymous browsing, the emphasis on privacy and security is far greater. Therefore, you must be very careful about which search engines you list with to ensure your site's anonymity and to avoid exposing it to harmful entities. Always choose reputable search engines that prioritize privacy and security to maintain the safety of both your site and your users.

Chapter 5: Securing Your Onion Site

Security Best Practices

Security best practices for a Linux server hosting an onion site are essential to ensure the safety of your data and users. Hardening your server should include configuring firewalls like ufw or iptables to limit access to necessary ports and services, as well as implementing SELinux or AppArmor for additional layers of security by enforcing strict access controls. Using HTTPS with your onion service is highly recommended to provide an encrypted connection, even though Tor already ensures anonymity and encryption; this additional layer protects data from potential threats between the Tor network and your application. It's also crucial to protect against common attacks like DDoS and brute-force attempts. To defend against DDoS, use services like Tor's built-in rate limiting or specialized Tor protection tools. Brute-force attacks can be mitigated by using strong passwords, implementing fail2ban to block suspicious IPs, and limiting login attempts. These practices help to safeguard your onion site from various threats and ensure a more secure and resilient environment.

For comprehensive guidance on securing your Linux servers, I highly recommend my book series, *The Linux Server Mastery Series*, available on Amazon. This series provides in-depth coverage of server hardening, security best practices, and practical solutions to help you build a secure and robust server environment.

Ensuring Anonymity

Unlike regular websites, an onion site doesn't require typical elements like meta tags, privacy statements, or policies in the same way. This is because onion sites, hosted on the Tor network, are designed to prioritize privacy and anonymity over traditional web practices. Meta tags, which are commonly used by search engines like Google to gather information and rank websites, are not necessary for **.onion** sites, since they don't rely on traditional search engines. Additionally, privacy policies and terms of service are typically aimed at ensuring compliance with legal regulations and protecting user data, but on the Tor network, the focus is on anonymity. Users are expected to access the site via the Tor browser, which inherently provides encryption and anonymity, reducing the need for extensive legal disclaimers or detailed personal information that would normally be required on surface web sites. While it's still a good practice to include some basic information for transparency, onion sites often don't need the same level of content focused on privacy and data protection, as Tor already addresses these concerns at the network level.

Keeping your identity separate from the onion site

Keeping your identity separate from your onion site is crucial for maintaining anonymity and ensuring that your activities cannot be traced back to you. Since onion sites are designed to provide privacy and security, it's important to avoid any actions or configurations that could inadvertently link your real-world identity to your **.onion** domain.

Here are several strategies to help maintain separation:

Use Pseudonyms and Anonymous Accounts: When registering domains, handling emails, or interacting with services related to your onion site, always use pseudonyms or anonymous accounts. Avoid using personal emails or identifiers that could be traced back to you. Create new, anonymous accounts specifically for managing your onion site to ensure that your real identity remains obscured.

Separate Hosting and Payment Methods: Do not host your onion site on servers or services where your personal details are required. Use payment methods like cryptocurrencies or anonymous prepaid cards to pay for hosting, and ensure your hosting provider accepts payments in a way that doesn't require personal identification. Additionally, ensure that the hosting provider doesn't require you to share any personal information during setup.

Use VPNs and Tor: Always use a VPN (Virtual Private Network) in combination with Tor when managing your onion site. This ensures that even if someone tries to trace your internet activity, it's much more difficult to link it to your physical location or identity. Avoid using your personal IP address for anything related to your onion site.

Limit Personal Identifiers: Ensure that there are no personal identifiers—such as names, locations, or photographs—on the website itself or in any interactions related to your onion site. Even small details, like an innocuous reference to your personal interests or specific times of activity, can be used to cross-reference and potentially identify you.

Secure Communication Channels: If you need to communicate with visitors or collaborators, use encrypted messaging services or email providers that don't require personal information, such as ProtonMail or Tutanota. Always ensure that your communication methods align with the principles of anonymity.

Avoiding metadata leaks from server and website

Avoiding metadata leaks from your server and website is critical for maintaining the privacy and anonymity of your onion site. Metadata—hidden data that can be embedded in files or communication logs—can inadvertently expose details about your site, server, or even your identity.

Here are several strategies to prevent metadata leaks:

Strip Metadata from Files: When uploading files (such as images, documents, or videos) to your server, be mindful that they may contain embedded metadata, such as timestamps, location data, or author information. Before uploading, use tools like exiftool or ImageOptim to remove this metadata. This helps ensure that no personal or identifying information is leaked along with your content.

Secure Server Logs: Server logs can contain sensitive information, including IP addresses, user-agent details, and timestamps that might be used to track visitors or identify patterns in traffic. To avoid these leaks, minimize the amount of logging your server performs, or configure it to log only essential information. You can also anonymize or purge logs regularly to further protect the privacy of users visiting your onion site.

Use Anonymous Hosting Services: To prevent server-related metadata leaks, consider using anonymous hosting providers that don't log personal details or IP addresses. Ensure that the provider has a strict no-logs policy and is based in a jurisdiction that does not mandate the collection or storage of user data.

Disable Unnecessary Services: Services like SSH, FTP, or even HTTP server status pages can sometimes expose unnecessary metadata that could be exploited. Disable or restrict these services unless absolutely necessary. If you do need them, ensure they are configured securely with proper access controls.

Minimize HTTP Headers: HTTP headers can sometimes contain identifying information, such as server software versions or technologies used. Use tools like ServerTokens in Apache or http_headers in Nginx to minimize or remove unnecessary headers from your site's response. This makes it more difficult for attackers to gather information about your server setup.

Content Delivery Networks (CDNs): While CDNs can provide performance benefits, they can also introduce metadata leaks if misconfigured, as they can log traffic and potentially expose your real IP address or the server hosting your onion site. If using a CDN, make sure it is privacy-friendly, such as one specifically designed for the Tor network, or consider avoiding CDNs altogether for maximum anonymity.

Avoid Personal Identifiers in Site Code: Metadata can also

exist in website code, such as comments, hidden fields, or in configuration files. Ensure that no personal information, usernames, or server details are embedded in the code of your site. Regularly audit your codebase for any unintended metadata or sensitive information.

Best practices for anonymous content management

Best practices for anonymous content management are essential for maintaining privacy, security, and the anonymity of both the site owner and visitors. Whether you are managing a blog, forum, or any other type of website, implementing the following strategies can help prevent identifying information from being exposed and protect both your data and users' privacy.

Use Pseudonyms and Anonymized Accounts: For both website management and content creation, always use pseudonyms and anonymous accounts. Avoid linking personal information to the content you manage, whether through your admin profile or any authorship details. Create email addresses, user accounts, and even social media profiles specifically for your website and its management.

Encrypt Communication Channels: Any communication between you and your team or visitors should be encrypted to prevent interception and data leaks. Use encrypted email services like ProtonMail or Tutanota, and ensure all communications on your website, especially if they involve user data or sensitive topics, are conducted through encrypted channels (like HTTPS or encrypted messaging platforms).

Regularly Review Content for Personal Identifiers: Always audit your content before publishing it to ensure there are no unintended personal identifiers that could link back to you or other individuals. This includes checking for direct or indirect mentions of your real name, location, IP address, or other personal details that may have slipped through, even in casual conversation or comments.

Ensure Content Anonymity for Contributors: If you accept contributions from others (such as guest posts, forum comments, or user-generated content), encourage contributors to use pseudonyms and avoid any personally identifiable information. Implement moderation policies that prevent users from revealing their real identities in comments or posts, which can compromise the anonymity of the site.

Limit the Use of Analytics: While tools like Google Analytics are useful for tracking traffic and user engagement, they can also collect identifying information, such as IP addresses and device details. Instead, consider using privacy-focused analytics tools like Matomo or GoatCounter, which provide insights without compromising user anonymity. If using analytics, be sure to anonymize IP addresses and avoid collecting unnecessary personal data.

Secure Content Management Systems (CMS): If you're using a CMS like WordPress, Joomla, or a custom platform, ensure that it is securely configured and regularly updated. Disable unnecessary plugins or modules that may leak information, and use security plugins or tools to monitor access and ensure the integrity of your content. Always follow best practices for securing your CMS against common vulnerabilities, such as using strong passwords and two-factor authentication.

Avoid Cross-Platform Linking: Do not link your onion site to other websites or services that require identifiable information (like social media accounts, personal blogs, or surface web platforms). Cross-linking to platforms that are not anonymous can lead to the inadvertent exposure of your identity or the site's activities.

Regular Backups and Safe Storage: Store backups of your site content in a secure and anonymous manner. Use encrypted storage solutions and avoid cloud services that require personal details. Regular backups ensure that you can recover your site in case of an attack or data loss without compromising your security.

Anonymous Hosting: Ensure that your hosting provider respects anonymity and does not require personal identification. Use anonymous payment methods like cryptocurrency to pay for hosting services and ensure your provider has a strict no-logs policy. Hosting your site with an anonymous provider will help ensure that your server details and data remain confidential.

Monitor for Data Leaks: Regularly audit your site for potential data leaks, such as exposure of personal information in site logs, error messages, or through improperly configured services. Set up security monitoring tools to alert you to any suspicious activity or attempts to expose your identity.

Chapter 6: Maintaining and Monitoring Your Onion Site

Monitoring Your Onion Site

Monitoring your onion site is crucial for maintaining its security, performance, and anonymity. Unlike regular websites, onion sites are often targeted by malicious actors seeking to exploit vulnerabilities. To ensure your site remains secure, regularly monitor server logs for unusual activity, such as unauthorized access attempts or high traffic spikes that may indicate a DDoS attack. Utilize security tools like Fail2ban to block malicious IP addresses and ensure your site's software is always up-to-date with the latest security patches. It's also important to monitor performance metrics, such as uptime and load times, to ensure your site is accessible to users without interruptions. Additionally, periodically review your site's content for potential leaks of personal information and ensure that no identifiable details are inadvertently exposed. By staying proactive with monitoring, you can detect potential threats early, ensuring that your onion site remains secure and functional.

Tools for monitoring uptime and server health

Monitoring uptime and server health is essential for ensuring that your onion site remains accessible and performs optimally. There are several tools available that help track your server's status, performance, and health in real-time.

Uptime Robot: This is a popular, free tool for monitoring website uptime. It checks your server every 5 minutes and alerts you if your site goes down. Uptime Robot supports monitoring of HTTP, HTTPS, and custom ports, making it suitable for both surface web and onion sites.

Netdata: Netdata is a comprehensive monitoring tool that provides real-time insights into your server's health, including CPU usage, memory, disk activity, network traffic, and more. It allows for the visualization of system metrics in an easy-to-read interface, helping you quickly identify potential issues and improve server performance.

Nagios: Nagios is an open-source monitoring system that is highly customizable. It allows you to monitor the health of your server, network, and applications. It provides detailed alerts for downtime, performance issues, and potential threats, making it a great option for administrators who need to manage large, complex systems.

Prometheus with Grafana: Prometheus is an open-source monitoring system and time series database that works well in conjunction with Grafana for visualizing server metrics. It provides detailed performance data, including uptime, server load, and resource usage, and can be used to monitor both the server and application levels.

Zabbix: Zabbix is another open-source monitoring tool that supports various metrics such as server performance, uptime, and application monitoring. It has the ability to create custom dashboards and reports and can send real-time notifications if your server or onion site goes down or experiences issues.

Pingdom: Pingdom is a reliable, cloud-based tool that allows you to monitor uptime, performance, and the response time of your onion site. It can be configured to check your site from multiple global locations, helping you ensure that your site remains accessible to users, no matter where they are located.

Monit: Monit is a lightweight tool designed for monitoring Unix-based systems, including uptime, memory usage, processes, and filesystems. It's highly customizable, providing alerts via email or other means when certain thresholds are exceeded, allowing administrators to take quick action.

Using analytics (without compromising anonymity)

Using analytics on an onion site can be tricky because traditional analytics tools like Google Analytics may compromise user anonymity. However, it's still possible to collect useful data about your site's performance and audience while maintaining privacy and security. The key is to use privacy-respecting, anonymous analytics tools that don't track personally identifiable information (PII) or expose your users to potential risks.

Matomo (formerly Piwik): Matomo is an open-source analytics platform that allows you to track site usage without compromising user privacy. By self-hosting Matomo, you retain full control over the data and can configure it to respect user anonymity, such as disabling IP address tracking and not using cookies. Matomo's customizable settings allow you to comply with privacy guidelines while still gathering useful insights, such as page views, bounce rates, and user demographics.

GoAccess: GoAccess is a real-time web log analyzer that can process server logs to provide insights into traffic, user behavior, and site performance. Since it only analyzes log files and doesn't require tracking users directly through scripts, it's an excellent tool for maintaining privacy while gathering useful analytics. It's especially suited for server admins who prefer not to implement additional client-side tracking mechanisms.

Simple Analytics: Simple Analytics is a privacy-focused analytics platform that doesn't rely on cookies or collect personal data. It provides basic metrics like page views, referrers, and devices used, all while ensuring user privacy. This platform is an excellent alternative for onion sites that want to monitor traffic without risking anonymity or violating privacy standards.

Fathom Analytics: Fathom Analytics is another privacy-respecting tool that doesn't track users or rely on cookies. It's designed to provide simple yet effective insights into website performance, including page views, popular pages, and referring sites. Fathom's approach focuses on respecting user privacy while still providing the site owner with relevant data.

Server-Side Log Analysis: For those who want the most privacy-respecting option, server-side log analysis can be an effective solution. By reviewing raw access logs, you can gather detailed information about traffic sources, user behavior, and page views without relying on external services. This method keeps all data on your server, preventing third-party trackers from accessing or analyzing your visitors' behavior.

When using analytics tools on an onion site, it's essential to configure them in a way that does not compromise the anonymity of your users. Always prioritize tools that respect privacy, avoid collecting personal data, and ensure that no identifying information is inadvertently shared. By doing so, you can still gain valuable insights into your site's performance while maintaining a strong commitment to privacy and security.

Backups and Disaster Recovery

Backups and disaster recovery are critical components of maintaining a secure and resilient onion site. Regularly backing up your server's data ensures that in the event of an attack, server failure, or other disaster, you can quickly restore your website and minimize downtime. It's important to use secure backup methods, such as encrypting backup files and storing them in off-site locations (preferably with redundancy). Automated backup tools can help ensure that backups are performed regularly without manual intervention. Additionally, implementing a disaster recovery plan that includes steps for server restoration, DNS configuration, and database recovery is essential for ensuring business continuity. By having a solid backup and recovery strategy in place, you can mitigate risks and ensure that your onion site remains operational, even in the face of unexpected challenges.

Best practices for backing up your onion site

Best practices for backing up your onion site involve ensuring that your backups are secure, reliable, and easily restorable. First and foremost, it's crucial to encrypt all backup files to protect sensitive data in case of theft or unauthorized access. Storing backups in multiple, geographically distributed locations, such as an off-site server or a secure cloud service, provides an added layer of redundancy. Regularly schedule automated backups to ensure that up-to-date copies of your site's files, databases, and configuration are always available. Use tools like rsync, Duplicity, or BorgBackup to automate and encrypt the backup process.

Another key practice is to back up not only the website content and databases but also critical configuration files, such as your web server and Tor service configurations, which are essential for restoring the site to its original state. Ensure that the backup process includes any SSL certificates, keys, and other sensitive credentials.

Test your backups periodically to confirm they can be restored quickly and accurately, as a backup is only as useful as its ability to be recovered. Additionally, consider keeping at least one backup that is not connected to the internet, to protect against ransomware or other cyberattacks that could potentially compromise cloud-based or local backups. Finally, monitor the backup process to ensure it runs correctly and without errors, so you're always prepared in case disaster strikes.

Restoring your site in case of a failure or attack

Restoring your onion site in the event of a failure or attack is a critical part of your disaster recovery plan. The first step is to assess the extent of the damage or breach, ensuring that the server and its backups have not been compromised. Once the situation is understood, begin by isolating the affected server to prevent further damage or unauthorized access. If an attack, such as a DDoS or a breach, is suspected, disconnecting the server from the network temporarily can help mitigate further impact.

To restore the site, retrieve the most recent backup, ensuring that it has been securely encrypted and stored offline or in a secure, off-site location. Restore the website's files, databases, and critical configuration files (including Tor and web server configurations) to the server, ensuring that you are working with clean, uncompromised versions of these files. If your server has been compromised, consider reinstalling the operating system to ensure no malicious files or backdoors remain. Once the restoration is complete, carefully reconfigure and test the web server, ensuring all configurations are intact and secure.

After the site is restored, conduct a thorough security audit to identify any vulnerabilities that may have been exploited during the attack. Update all software, patch any security holes, and change any compromised credentials, such as SSH keys, Tor hidden service keys, and database passwords. It's also advisable to review logs for signs of the attack and implement enhanced security measures, such as firewall rules, intrusion detection systems, and rate limiting, to prevent future incidents.

Finally, once the site is live again, monitor it closely for unusual activity, and inform your users of any potential disruptions. Maintaining a regular backup and testing process can significantly reduce downtime and help ensure that your onion site remains resilient against future failures or attacks.

Chapter 7: Legal and Ethical Considerations

Legal Implications of Running an Onion Site

Running an onion site comes with important legal and ethical considerations that vary depending on the nature of the content and the jurisdiction in which you operate. While the anonymity provided by the Tor network can help protect your identity and privacy, it does not shield you from legal responsibilities. Law enforcement agencies are increasingly capable of detecting the use of Tor and even identifying Tor users through methods like traffic analysis and fingerprinting techniques, which can undermine the assumption of complete anonymity. Hosting illegal content, such as illicit drugs, weapons, or stolen data, can lead to criminal charges, even if the site is hosted on the dark web.

It's crucial to understand the laws in your country regarding online activities, including privacy, data protection, and content regulation. Ethically, operators of onion sites should be cautious about promoting harm or engaging in illegal activities, ensuring that the site serves legitimate purposes and respects user privacy. Legal risks can be mitigated by operating within the bounds of the law, using encryption to protect sensitive data, and ensuring that the site's activities are transparent and accountable while respecting the privacy and safety of users.

Understanding local and international laws about anonymity and privacy

Understanding local and international laws regarding anonymity and privacy is essential when operating an onion site, as these laws can vary significantly across jurisdictions. In many countries, the use of anonymizing tools like Tor is legal, but certain activities conducted anonymously, such as distributing illegal content or engaging in fraud, are not. It's crucial to be aware of the specific laws related to privacy, data protection, and online behavior in your own country, as well as in the countries where your users may reside. For example, in the European Union, the General Data Protection Regulation (GDPR) places strict rules on how personal data must be handled, including the right to be forgotten and data access requests, even for anonymous online services.

Similarly, some countries have laws that target individuals or organizations that facilitate illegal activities, even if those activities are conducted under the guise of anonymity. International treaties and cooperation between governments can also influence how cases of online crime are investigated and prosecuted, potentially leading to legal action against individuals operating onion sites. Therefore, operators of onion sites should be cautious and fully understand their legal responsibilities, including potential risks related to privacy laws, surveillance, and cross-border law enforcement. It's important to consult legal experts if you're unsure about the regulations that apply to your site's operations, as failure to comply with laws can result in serious legal consequences.

Common legal risks of hosting a dark web service

Hosting a dark web service comes with several common legal risks that operators should be aware of, particularly because the anonymity of the dark web can attract illegal activities. One of the most significant risks is the hosting of illegal content. Many dark web services facilitate the exchange of illicit materials, including drugs, weapons, counterfeit goods, and stolen data, all of which can result in serious criminal charges for the service operator, even if they do not directly participate in the transactions. Another risk is the facilitation of illegal activities such as hacking, fraud, or money laundering, where operators might be held liable for enabling or profiting from these crimes. Even if the operator is not directly involved in illegal actions, they may still face charges under conspiracy or aiding and abetting laws.

Moreover, privacy laws present another challenge. Many jurisdictions have strict regulations concerning the handling of personal data. While the Tor network provides anonymity, operators of dark web services still need to be cautious about collecting, storing, or processing personal data. Failure to comply with data protection regulations, such as the European Union's General Data Protection Regulation (GDPR), can lead to heavy fines and penalties, even if the data collection was unintentional or seemingly anonymous.

The dark web itself, including the Tor network, was initially created by the U.S. government's CIA for the purpose of protecting communications and providing secure anonymity for intelligence operations. However, its evolution has led to its use for both legal and illegal purposes. Law enforcement agencies are continuously improving their capabilities to track and infiltrate dark web operations. Using advanced techniques such as traffic analysis, malware, or informants, authorities can sometimes uncover the identities of service operators or users, leading to legal action. Lastly, operators of dark web services might face legal consequences simply by hosting or distributing content that violates copyright or intellectual property laws. Even though such services operate outside the surface web, intellectual property holders may still pursue legal action.

To mitigate these risks, it is essential for operators to have a solid understanding of the laws that apply to them, including local, national, and international regulations, and to ensure their activities are compliant with applicable legal standards. Consulting legal professionals who specialize in cybersecurity and internet law is also advisable to avoid unintentional legal violations.

Ethical Use of the Dark Web

How to promote ethical behavior on your onion site

Promoting ethical behavior on your onion site is essential for ensuring that it serves a positive and legitimate purpose, even within the anonymity of the dark web. The Tor network and onion sites, by design, provide privacy and protection against surveillance, but with this anonymity comes responsibility. As an operator of an onion site, it is important to create a space where users can engage in lawful and ethical activities, avoiding the facilitation or promotion of harm.

To promote ethical behavior, start by establishing clear guidelines for acceptable content and activities on your site. These guidelines should explicitly prohibit illegal actions such as trafficking in illicit goods, exploiting others, or engaging in cybercrime. Implement strong content moderation practices to ensure that illegal or harmful content is swiftly removed, and consider using technologies or services that can help identify and block malicious users or activities. By creating a code of conduct and consistently enforcing it, you can foster an environment that encourages lawful behavior.

Additionally, consider the ethical implications of the data you collect. Avoid storing or sharing personally identifiable information unless absolutely necessary, and ensure that any data you handle is managed in accordance with privacy best practices. As an ethical operator, it is crucial to avoid exploiting the anonymity of the dark web for illegal financial gain, harmful actions, or activities that could negatively impact others.

Finally, transparency and accountability are key in maintaining ethical standards. Clearly communicate to your users what the site stands for and how it operates. Create a system for reporting unethical behavior and be open to feedback from the community. By promoting transparency, you can help users trust that your onion site operates with integrity, making it a safer and more responsible part of the dark web.

Promoting ethical behavior on an onion site involves setting clear expectations, enforcing guidelines, and prioritizing privacy and safety while staying compliant with both the law and ethical standards. By doing so, you can ensure that your site contributes positively to the dark web's ecosystem and serves the greater good.

Balancing anonymity with responsible content management

Balancing anonymity with responsible content management is a critical challenge when operating an onion site on the dark web. The core appeal of the Tor network and onion services lies in their ability to provide strong privacy and anonymity for both site operators and users. However, this anonymity can be a double-edged sword, as it can also shield malicious actors who wish to engage in illegal or harmful activities. As an operator, it is important to uphold privacy and anonymity while also ensuring that the content hosted on your site adheres to ethical and legal standards.

One way to strike this balance is by creating a clear set of guidelines for acceptable content and behavior. While maintaining user anonymity, these guidelines should outline what types of content are prohibited, such as illegal goods, services, or activities that promote harm. To enforce these guidelines, operators should use strong content moderation tools to monitor and filter user-generated content without violating privacy. This could involve implementing automated systems that detect prohibited content, such as images or keywords related to illegal activities, while respecting user anonymity as much as possible.

At the same time, it is essential to be transparent with users about the site's policies and how their anonymity is being protected. Users should feel confident that their identity is not at risk when engaging with the site, but they should also be aware that illegal activities will not be tolerated. Striking the right balance means educating users about responsible use of the site and establishing an environment where both anonymity and lawful behavior coexist.

Another important aspect is data management. While it's crucial to safeguard the anonymity of users, site operators must also be mindful of the data they collect and store. Limiting data collection to what is strictly necessary and employing robust encryption techniques can help prevent unintentional leaks that might compromise user anonymity. Additionally, operators should be aware of data retention practices, making sure that sensitive information is not kept longer than necessary.

Ultimately, balancing anonymity with responsible content management requires a commitment to both privacy and ethical standards. By setting clear guidelines, using effective moderation, and practicing responsible data management, you can help ensure that your onion site remains a safe, ethical, and law-abiding space for users, while still preserving the core value of anonymity that makes the Tor network so unique.

Appendices

Appendix A - Recommended & Ethical Dark Websites

When exploring the dark web, it is important to prioritize ethical websites that contribute positively to privacy, security, and the protection of personal information. While the dark web has a reputation for hosting illicit activities, it also offers a range of resources that promote free speech, privacy, and secure communication, often providing refuge for individuals living under oppressive regimes or for those in need of anonymity for legitimate reasons.

Here are some recommended and ethical dark websites to explore:

ProPublica (propublica3fryh6bhx.onion) ProPublica is an investigative news organization that has a dark web presence to offer a more secure and anonymous way for whistleblowers and others to access information. The site provides investigative journalism that promotes transparency and accountability.

The Intercept (theinterceptiwwfyt2pk4t2k46r.onion) The Intercept is known for its focus on national security, privacy, and government surveillance. The site has an onion address

to facilitate secure and anonymous access for those interested in privacy, cybersecurity, and civil liberties.

SecureDrop (securedrop.org) SecureDrop is a platform used by journalists and media organizations to securely receive documents from whistleblowers and other sources. It is designed to protect the identities of those who contribute sensitive information. Many media outlets, including The New York Times, use SecureDrop for secure communication with anonymous sources.

Liberty Reserve (libertyreserve.onion) Liberty Reserve is a privacy-focused digital currency platform for individuals seeking to avoid surveillance or censorship. Its presence on the dark web helps facilitate anonymous financial transactions.

DuckDuckGo (duckduckgoonion.com) DuckDuckGo is a privacy-respecting search engine that does not track users' search history or personal information. Its dark web version offers users the ability to search the internet anonymously while ensuring their privacy is maintained.

Tor Project (expyuzz4wqqyqhjn.onion) The Tor Project's official website provides resources, updates, and information about the Tor network itself, which is a vital tool for users seeking online anonymity. The Tor Project's dark web presence helps ensure that users can access this important information securely.

Riseup (riseup.net) Riseup is an activist organization that offers encrypted email and other secure services for activists, journalists, and others who need privacy. It's known for its strong stance on privacy and data security, and its services are widely respected within activist communities.

OnionShare (onionshare.org) OnionShare is a free and open-source tool that allows users to securely share files over the Tor network. It helps maintain anonymity and offers a safe way to transfer files without revealing any personal information.

While exploring the dark web, it's critical to verify the legitimacy of sites you visit. Always ensure that websites and services align with ethical standards and avoid those that engage in illegal or harmful activities. Remember that while the dark web provides enhanced privacy and anonymity, it also comes with risks, and users should take appropriate precautions to protect themselves.

Appendix B – Dark Web Criminal Activities Exposed

Ross Ulbricht – Silk Road

Ross Ulbricht, the creator of Silk Road, operated one of the most infamous dark web marketplaces, facilitating the sale of drugs, weapons, and other illicit goods.

Arrest: Ulbricht was arrested in 2013 by the FBI in San Francisco. He was convicted on multiple charges, including conspiracy to commit money laundering and drug trafficking.

Outcome: Sentenced to life in prison without the possibility of parole.

Alexandre Cazes – AlphaBay

AlphaBay, run by Alexandre Cazes, was a large dark web marketplace for illegal drugs, firearms, stolen data, and counterfeit goods. It was regarded as the largest dark web marketplace before its shutdown.

Arrest: Cazes was arrested in 2017 in Thailand as part of an international law enforcement operation. His laptop was seized while it was still logged into the AlphaBay administration panel.

Outcome: Cazes was found dead in his prison cell, allegedly by suicide, shortly after his arrest.

Matthew Phan – Dark Web Weapons Dealer

Matthew Phan, a Canadian man, used the dark web to purchase firearms and other illegal items.

Arrest: Phan was arrested in 2018 after law enforcement tracked his illegal purchases. They found evidence linking him to the purchase of handguns, a rifle, and drugs via the dark web.

Outcome: In 2019, he was sentenced to 15 years in prison for drug trafficking and firearms offenses.

Gal Vallerius – Dark Web Drug Dealer (OxyMonster)

Gal Vallerius, known by his pseudonym "OxyMonster," was a French dark web drug dealer who sold prescription opioids on Dream Market.

Arrest: Vallerius was arrested in 2017 upon arriving in the U.S. to compete in a beard competition. Authorities identified him as OxyMonster through his Bitcoin transactions and social media activity.

Outcome: Vallerius pleaded guilty to drug distribution and money laundering and was sentenced to 20 years in prison.

Aaron Shamo – Fentanyl Kingpin

Aaron Shamo led an online drug operation selling counterfeit prescription pills laced with fentanyl on the dark web.

Arrest: Shamo was arrested in 2016 in Utah after law enforcement traced large-scale fentanyl shipments to his home, which he used as a base of operations.

Outcome: In 2019, Shamo was convicted of running a drug trafficking organization and sentenced to life in prison.

Richard Castro – Bitcoin Launderer

Richard Castro, known as "Chems_usa," was involved in laundering Bitcoin and selling synthetic opioids, including fentanyl, on the dark web.

Arrest: Castro was arrested in 2019 after investigators linked him to laundering $1.5 million worth of Bitcoin through his illegal activities.

Outcome: He pleaded guilty to money laundering and narcotics distribution and faced a significant prison sentence.

Eric Marques – Freedom Hosting Child Exploitation Case

Eric Marques, an Irishman, ran Freedom Hosting, a major provider of dark web services, many of which were involved in child exploitation content.

Arrest: Marques was arrested in 2013 in Ireland, following a joint operation by the FBI and Irish police. He was responsible for hosting numerous dark web sites related to child pornography.

Outcome: Extradited to the U.S., Marques pleaded guilty in 2019 to conspiracy to advertise child pornography and faces up to 30 years in prison.

Galvin Ryan – Identity Theft

Galvin Ryan used the dark web to buy and sell stolen personal information, including social security numbers and credit card details.

Arrest: He was arrested after investigators tracked fraudulent activity to his dark web transactions.

Outcome: Ryan was convicted of identity theft, fraud, and cybercrimes, serving multiple years in prison.

Ringleader of Wall Street Market

Wall Street Market was one of the largest dark web marketplaces for drugs, weapons, and stolen data.

Arrest: In 2019, the German authorities arrested three individuals believed to be the administrators of the marketplace after an undercover operation. The group was also involved in an exit scam, stealing money from users before the platform shut down.

Outcome: The administrators were charged with running an illegal online marketplace, drug trafficking, and money laundering.

Peter Scully – Child Exploitation Ring

Peter Scully ran a notorious dark web child exploitation ring, producing and distributing horrific child abuse material through hidden services.

Arrest: Scully was arrested in 2015 in the Philippines after a global manhunt and investigation into his dark web activities.

Outcome: In 2018, Scully was sentenced to life in prison, with additional charges still pending.

Appendix C – Great ideas for Ethical Dark Web Sites

While the dark web is often associated with illicit activities, it also holds potential for promoting privacy, freedom of expression, and secure communications. Ethical dark web sites can serve a variety of legitimate purposes, benefiting individuals in restrictive regions or those seeking privacy. Here are some ideas for ethical dark web sites:

Whistleblowing Platforms

Websites like **SecureDrop** and **GlobaLeaks** enable whistleblowers to submit sensitive information securely and anonymously. These platforms protect users' identities while allowing them to expose corruption, human rights violations, or corporate malfeasance without fear of retaliation. Encouraging the use of encrypted, anonymous submission methods helps maintain integrity in exposing injustices.

Human Rights Advocacy Sites

The dark web can serve as a safe space for human rights organizations, journalists, and activists. Platforms like **TorLeaks** offer tools for secure communication and data sharing, particularly for those living in countries with restrictive or oppressive regimes. These sites provide a vital service by offering a censorship-free environment where people can organize and share their findings without fear of government surveillance.

Secure Communication Tools for Activists

Websites like **Tutanota** or **ProtonMail**, which provide encrypted email services, can be extended to the dark web, offering secure channels for activists working in dangerous environments. These platforms ensure that sensitive information remains private and prevents third parties from gaining access to critical communication between human rights defenders, journalists, and their supporters.

Privacy-Focused Search Engines

DuckDuckGo or **Startpage** offer privacy-focused search engine capabilities and could be adapted for use on the dark web, allowing users to search for information anonymously. These types of sites help mitigate tracking and data collection, preserving the user's privacy while searching for legitimate, public information without leaving a trace.

Decentralized Marketplaces for Goods & Services (with Monitoring or Private Business-Only User Access)

Decentralized marketplaces offer users the ability to engage in transactions without relying on a central authority, ensuring privacy and security. To foster ethical practices, these platforms can implement monitoring systems or limit access to verified business accounts only. Such measures help mitigate illegal activities while maintaining the privacy of legitimate users. By combining the benefits of decentralization with ethical oversight or business-only participation, these marketplaces can operate securely and responsibly.

Decentralized Marketplaces for Digital Goods

Digital goods, like art, research, or educational content, can be shared in a secure, anonymous way. Platforms that facilitate this type of exchange allow individuals to access resources freely while ensuring privacy. These platforms should adhere to strict guidelines, ensuring no illegal content is uploaded, creating a space for education and learning while avoiding censorship.

Open-Source Software Repositories

Open-source software is central to ethical dark web usage, with sites like **GitHub** offering repositories that can be mirrored on the dark web. These platforms promote free, transparent software development and allow programmers in restrictive environments to access and contribute to global coding projects without fear of surveillance.

www.ingramcontent.com/pod-product-compliance
Lightning Source LLC
La Vergne TN
LVHW051336050326
832903LV00031B/3569